FIRST BOOK OF GRASSES

THE STRUCTURE OF GRASSES EXPLAINED FOR BEGINNERS

BY

AGNES CHASE

ASSISTANT AGROSTOLOGIST, UNITED STATES DEPARTMENT OF AGRICULTURE

New York

THE MACMILLAN COMPANY

1922

Set up and electrotyped. Published November, 1922.

Printed in the United States of America

PREFACE

Of all plants grasses are the most important to man. The different kinds are known by very few even among botanists. This is largely because they are supposed to be very difficult. When the structure of grasses is clearly understood, they are not more difficult to study than are other plants. The method here offered has been used by the author for some years in teaching special students.

The introduction explains the method followed. The body of the primer consists of twelve lessons, graded from the simplest to the most complex. Each lesson is accompanied by figures bringing out the facts in the text. The difference in the size of the flowering organs is so great that the figures are not drawn to the same scale. The organs are enlarged as much as necessary to illustrate the character discussed.

Grasses of the United States are used for the lessons and the commoner ones are selected so far as possible; however, our native grasses cover so wide a range that the principles laid down in the lessons are applicable to grasses generally.

AGNES CHASE.

Washington, D. C., *August 10, 1922.*

TABLE OF CONTENTS

LIST OF ILLUSTRATIONS

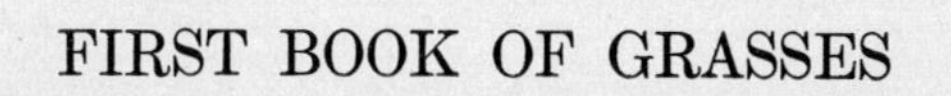

FIRST BOOK OF GRASSES

FIRST BOOK OF GRASSES

INTRODUCTION

The purpose of this primer is to give those with little or no knowledge of botany such an understanding of the structure of grasses as will enable them to use manuals of botany and other technical works, to the end that our native grasses may become better known and their worth and beauty be more fully appreciated.

The best method of studying any organisms is to observe and examine the organisms themselves. Since these can not be provided in a book, drawings of the objects studied are here offered as the best substitute. These drawings are purposely somewhat diagrammatic in order to bring out particular characters that may be less prominent in the actual plants. While the drawings convey clearer ideas of structure than can words and are to be used constantly with the text, they can but inadequately take the place of the plants themselves. The student, therefore, should collect for study as many different kinds of living grasses as possible.

The idea of a primer has been kept in mind. The subject is presented as simply as possible, and only enough grasses are examined in each lesson to illustrate the different modifications and to prepare the student to comprehend the greater modifications shown in subsequent lessons.

The classification of grasses, that is, the grouping together of related forms, is based on the characters of the aggregate of minute flowers and bracts known as the *spikelet.* It is necessary, therefore, for anyone who wishes to be able to identify a given grass to understand the structure and modifications of the spikelet. This primer is really an elementary study of the morphology of the spikelet. [Morphology is a branch of science that treats of form and structure. The study of the morphology of the spikelet enables one to recognize its various organs under whatever form they may assume.]

USE OF TECHNICAL TERMS

Many persons who might otherwise make an effort to learn something about our common wild flowers and trees, as well as grasses, are deterred by the sight of the unfamiliar words used in botanical descriptions. This supposed lion in the way, if one will but draw near enough to see, is only a "harmless necessary cat." No boy learns a trade, no girl learns to sew without learning the names of the tools used. Words like hames, whippletree, terrets, and a hundred more, meaningless to the city-bred rider on a trolley-car, are familiar terms to the farmer.[1] Such

[1] Mark Twain's description (in "A Tramp Abroad") of how they hitch horses in Europe is a good example of the con-

terms as carburetor, accelerator, clutch, spark-plug or magneto, unknown a few years ago, are now understood by nearly everyone, and those who do not as yet understand these terms are by no means deterred thereby from buying (or wishing for) an automobile. Spikelet, glume, and lemma are words no more difficult to learn than are hames, crupper, or whippletree, carburetor, clutch, or magneto. The reason for using these botanical terms is the same as that for using the names of the different parts of a harness; they are simpler and more exact than would be a descriptive phrase. It is simpler to say "terrets" than to say "the rings that stick up in the middle of the harness on the horse's back that you pass the reins through" and it is simpler to say

fusion caused by want of technical terms: "The man stands up the horses on each side of the thing that projects from the front end of the wagon, throws the gear on top of the horses, and passes the thing that goes forward through a ring, and hauls it aft, and passes the other thing through the other ring and hauls it aft on the other side of the other horse, opposite to the first one, after crossing them and bringing the loose end back, and then buckles the other thing underneath the horse, and takes another thing and wraps it around the thing I spoke of before, and puts another thing over each horse's head, and puts the iron thing in his mouth, and brings the ends of these things aft over his back, after buckling another one around under his neck, and hitching another thing on a thing that goes over his shoulders, and then takes the slack of the thing which I mentioned a while ago and fetches it aft and makes it fast to the thing that pulls the wagon, and hands the other things up to the driver."

"glume" when speaking of that organ of a grass than to say "the little green scale on the outside of the thing with the seed in it."

In the first lesson nearly all the new words that a study of grasses will require are explained and illustrated by figures. The few additional terms necessary are explained as they are used. No attempt is made to write a primer of grasses in words of one syllable nor to produce a work on "how to know the grasses" without mental effort. It can not be done.

USE OF LATIN NAMES

Besides unfamiliar terms there are the unfamiliar Latin names of the plants which some hesitate to encounter. But many of the names in common use for trees and herbs are the botanical names. Magnolia, Rhododendron, Petunia, Asparagus, Chrysanthemum, Phlox are the Latin botanical names and are freely used by all without hesitation. Panicum, Paspalum, Bromus, Festuca, Hordeum are no more difficult. As in the case of such terms as glume and lemma, the Latin names of plants are used for the sake of exactness. Common names of plants, especially of those which are useful, troublesome, or conspicuous, are more definitely applied in older countries where the inhabitants have dwelt in a region for many generations than they are with us. Our ancestors brought names of old world plants with them to their new homes and applied them to plants something like the familiar ones. Consequently, many common names are used in different parts of the country for widely different plants. In Illinois "June-grass" is Kentucky blue-grass (*Poa pratensis*), a valuable pasture grass; in Maine "June-grass" is *Danthonia spicata*, an almost worthless little relative of wild oats; and in parts of the West it is *Kœleria cristata*. The name "blue-joint" is used for three very unlike grasses. On the other hand, many plants have different names in separate parts of the country. Around Washington, D. C., for example, Azalea is commonly called "honey-suckle." Many economic plants (such as potato, turnip, and rye) have common names uniform in any one language but different in distinct languages. When the Latin name of a plant is used, it is definitely understood not only throughout the United States but throughout the world what species is referred to. However, the primary reason for using the botanical names is that these indicate the relationship of the plants. All plants of a *kind* have the same genus (or generic) name. [Genus is the singular, genera the plural, generic the adjective.] Kentucky blue-grass and all its kind are Poa: *P. pratensis*, *P. trivialis*, *P. annua*, *P. Sandbergii*, and so on. The common names of these, Kentucky blue-grass or June-grass, rough meadow-grass, spear-grass, little bunch-grass, respectively, give no clue to their relationship or kind. Knowing *Poa pratensis* anyone hearing of any grass named Poa has an idea of what it is like; it is something like *Poa pratensis*. Some common names, especially those of trees, indicate the kind: Oak, with black, white, scarlet, swamp, and post oak, for example, and also hickory and ash; but for herbs, and especially grasses, the common name usually gives no indication of the kind of plant it refers to. Often the name is misleading. Rib-grass is not a grass, but a plantain; poison ivy is not an ivy, but a sumach. To convey definite ideas we must use definite terms and definite names.

TOOLS NEEDED

Any work that one engages in requires tools. For the study of grasses we need but few. Grass flowers are too small to be seen distinctly with the naked eye. A lens magnifying about ten diameters is necessary. This may be mounted on a stand or it may be a hand lens. A simple dissecting microscope with two or three lenses of different magnification would be more convenient and would well repay the cost, but it is not absolutely necessary. If one has only a hand lens, an eye-piece, such as watchmakers place in the eye, will also be found very useful in dissecting, as it leaves both hands free. One or two dissecting needles are needed. These can be made by forcing the heads of coarse sewing needles into a pencil-shaped piece of soft wood. After some practice one learns to use the nail of the left forefinger skilfully in dissecting. One can work more rapidly with this and one needle than with a pair of needles. A scalpel is useful, but the small sharp blade of a penknife will answer instead. It is well to have a piece of black paper or cardboard on which to place hairy spikelets. The hairs on the different parts show up well against this background.

It is the aim to use, so far as possible, the characters that may be seen in the different parts of the spikelet with but little dissection. When further dissection is necessary, instructions will be given at the end of the lesson requiring it.

LESSON I

THE GRASS FAMILY

To most persons grass is almost any green vegetation of rather low growth, especially such as may be grazed. To the student of plants, a grass is a member of the natural family Poaceæ, or Gramineæ, distinguished by its structure.

Grasses are herbs with round or flattened (never 3-angled), usually hollow stems (**culms**) solid at the joints (**nodes**), and 2-ranked, alternate, parallel-veined leaves, composed of two parts, the **sheath,** which surrounds the culm like a tube split down one side, and the **blade,** which is usually strap-shaped, flat, folded, or with rolled margins. At the junction of the sheath and blade, on the inside, is a small appendage (the **ligule**); this is commonly thin in texture; sometimes it is only a ring of hairs, rarely it is obsolete. The plants may be annual or perennial. The root, stem, and leaves are the vegetative part of the plant (Fig. 1). These are all that are concerned with the life of the individual plant. The flowers have to do with perpetuating the species. In grasses the vegetative parts are more uniform and characteristic than in most other families.

Having stem and leaves of any plant, it can always be readily decided whether or not it is a grass. The

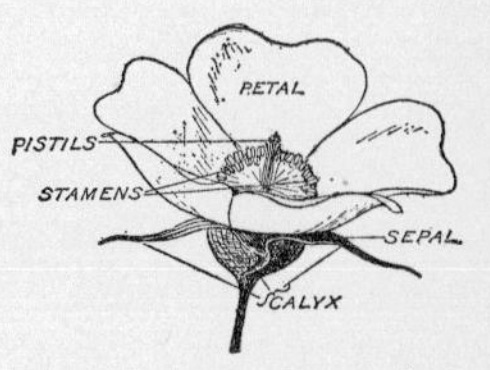

FIG. 2. Typical complete flower, showing calyx, corolla, stamens and pistils.

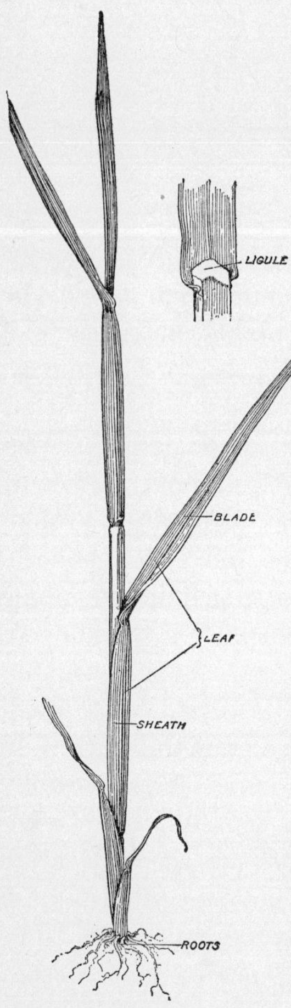

FIG. 1. Vegetative part of a grass plant; part of leaf opened out.

only plants that may reasonably be mistaken for grasses are the sedges. In these the culms are solid or pithy, are not jointed, and are commonly 3-sided; the leaves are always 3-ranked, and the sheaths always closed.

The flowers of grasses are small and inconspicuous. They consist of a single pistil with a 1-celled, 1-ovuled ovary, two styles, each with a feathery stigma, and three (rarely one or six) stamens with delicate filaments and 2-celled anthers. Two minute scales, called lodicules, situated back of the pistil, at blooming time become turgid and force open the enveloping scales.

In Fig. 2 are shown the parts of a common flower

(the wild prairie rose with long styles). The calyx and corolla are the floral envelopes; the **stamens** and **pistils** are the essential organs of a flower, the parts that produce seed. The floral envelopes protect the essential organs in the bud and, by secreting nectar which attracts insects or in other ways, commonly aid in securing the fertilization of the flower. The **pistil** consists of the ovary, style, and stigma. The **ovary** contains the ovules, which when fertilized develop into the seeds. The **style** serves to lift the stigma into the air. The **stigma** is more or less expanded, has a viscid surface to which the pollen-grains adhere and upon which they germinate, sending their contents in a minute tube which pushes down through the style to the ovules, fertilizing them.

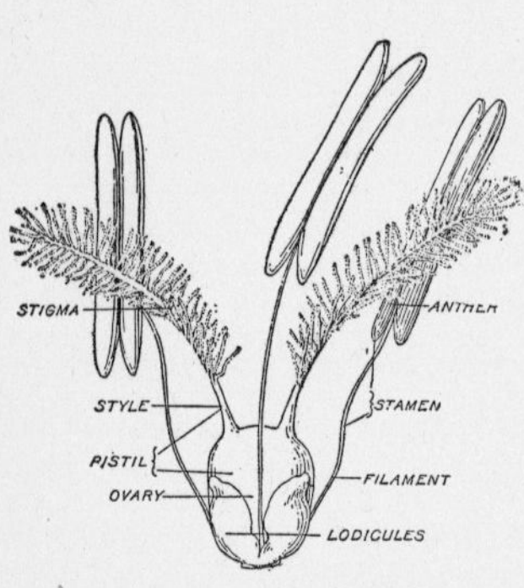

Fig. 3. Grass flower, showing stamens and pistil and the rudiments of floral envelope.

The grass flower (Fig. 3) is reduced to the essential organs, the floral envelopes being represented by the minute **lodicules.** Each flower is borne in the axil of a small green bract (the **lemma**) and is subtended and enveloped in a second bract (the **palea**). The flower with its lemma and palea is termed the **floret** (Fig. 4). The ripened ovary (the **grain,** or **caryopsis)** (Fig. 5) consists of a small **embryo** lying at the base of a mass of starchy **endosperm.** [Endosperm means within the sperm or seed. It is the store of food used by the infant plantlet when it begins to grow.] The "germ" of a kernel of corn is the embryo, while the remainder of the kernel is starchy endosperm. The grain lies in the palea with the **hilum** (the scar of the point of attachment) toward it, and the embryo on the side toward the lemma. Fig. 5 gives two views of a grain, one showing the hilum, the other the embryo. In Fig. 81, A (page 91), are two kernels of corn showing the embryos. The grain with very few exceptions is permanently inclosed in the lemma and palea, the mature floret being the **fruit,** that is, the seed with its permanent envelopes. The florets are borne in two ranks and alternate upon an axis (the **rachilla**). Below them are two bracts without flowers (the **glumes**). The glumes, rachilla, and florets together form the **spikelet.**

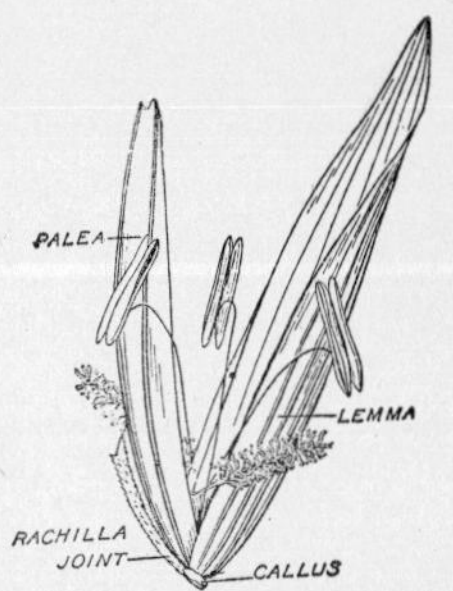

Fig. 4. A floret at flowering time.

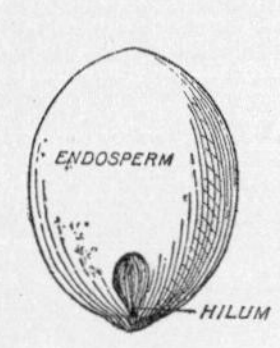

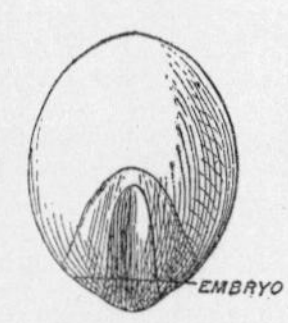

Fig. 5. Two views of a grain.

Fig. 6 is a diagram of a branch with leaves and flowers arranged as are the glumes, lemmas, paleas, and flowers of a grass spikelet. Fig. 7 is a diagram of a spikelet for comparison with Fig. 6. [The hypothetical flower-bearing branchlet is *never* elongate, as here shown for the sake of comparison. The palea is immediately above the lemma and the flower immediately above the palea.] It will be seen that the spikelet is theoretically a leafy flowering branch with a jointed main axis, the flowers, except

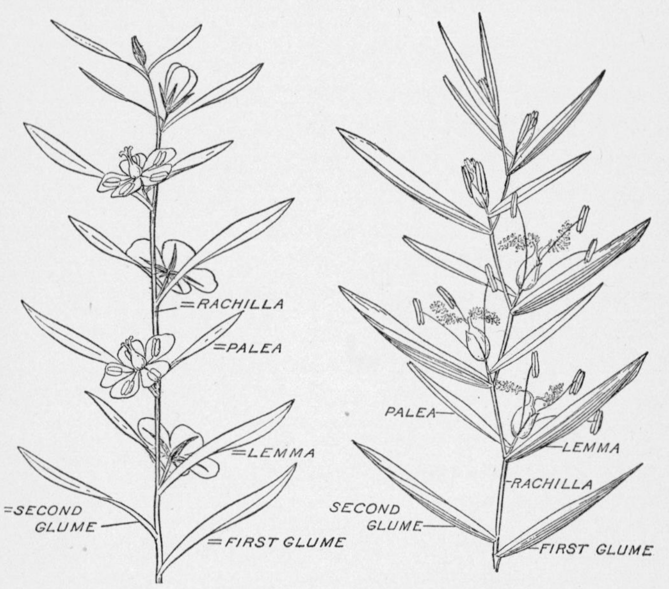

Fig. 6. Diagram of a flowering branch.

Fig. 7. Diagram of a grass spikelet.

for the minute lodicules, reduced to the essential organs. In Fig. 8 a typical grass spikelet is shown, the lemmas and paleas nearly closed together and concealing the flowers.

The spikelet is characteristic of grasses and is not found in any other family except that of the sedges.

In the spikelets of sedges the florets are commonly, but not always, spirally arranged, there never is a palea, and the fruit is an achene or nutlet. [The "seeds" of buttercups and mints are achenes or nutlets.]

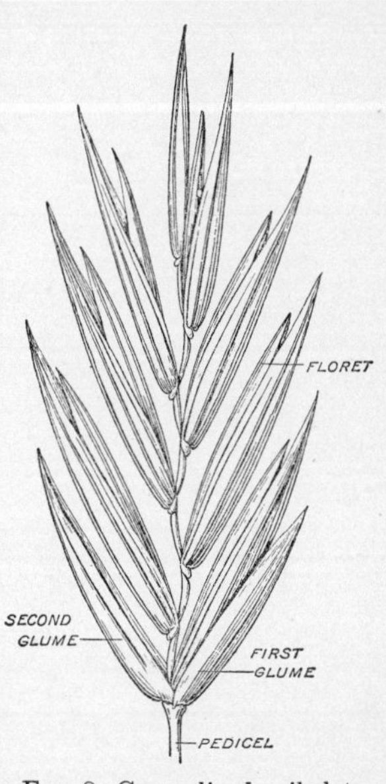

FIG. 8. Generalized spikelet.

In grasses specialization takes place mostly in the spikelet. By its vegetative characters we know a given plant to be a grass, but it is by its spikelets and their arrangement that we know what kind of a grass it is. The genera of grasses and the groups of genera called tribes are based on the structure of the spikelets and their arrangement in the inflorescence.

Before studying the spikelet we must observe the relatively few specializations of the vegetative parts. As in other plants, stems or parts of stems may be underground. These underground stems (**rhizomes,** or rootstocks) are borne at the base of the main culm under the earth, spread out horizontally, and in due time send up shoots which form young plants at a distance from the parent. Sod-forming grasses have this kind of underground stem. Kentucky blue-grass (*Poa pratensis*, Fig. 9) furnishes an excellent example. Sometimes the rhizome is thick and woody, sending up shoots from its nodes, the whole forming a dense colony, as in gama-grass (*Tripsacum dactyloides*). A rhizome, being a stem, is jointed and bears scales, which are reduced leaves. By these it may always be distinguished from a root, which is not jointed and never bears scales. In some grasses the shoots borne at the base of the culm are on the surface of the earth instead of beneath it. Such shoots are **stolons,** or runners. These, like rhizomes, are jointed and bear scales or, sometimes, well-developed leaves. Rhizomes and stolons both bear roots at the under side of the nodes. In a few species, Bermuda-grass for one, a plant may produce either rhizomes or stolons according to the conditions under which it is growing. There is no real difference between a rhizome and a stolon, the one is below ground and colorless, the other above ground and green.

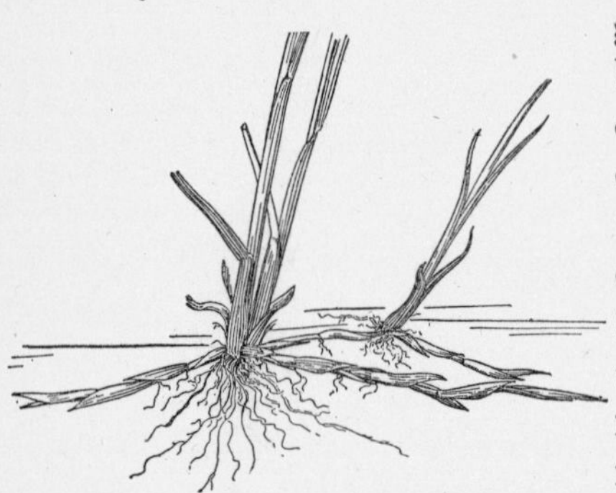

Fig. 9. Base of plant and underground parts, roots and rhizomes, of *Poa pratensis.*

Culms are hollow in most grasses, but in corn, sugar-cane, sorghum, and related grasses they are pithy. They may be erect, spreading, or creeping; they may be simple or freely branching. A branch is borne only at a node in the axil of a sheath, that is, between the sheath and the culm. It either grows up parallel with the parent culm until it emerges from the sheath or the young branch splits the sheath and grows outward. In manuals of botany these two methods of branching are called **intravaginal,** that is, inside the vagina (Latin for sheath), and **extravaginal,** outside the sheath. In bunch-grasses, like orchard-grass and the wheat-grasses of the West, the branching is intravaginal; in Kentucky blue-grass, quack-grass, and others producing rhizomes or stolons, the branching is extravaginal. The branches borne at the middle and upper nodes of a culm are nearly always intravaginal. If they spread from the parent culm they do not burst through the sheath but carry it with them.

Leaves are always borne at the nodes and are always 2-ranked (see Fig. 1, page 9). In corn and other large grasses the leaves sometimes appear to be all on one side instead of 2-ranked. This is due to a twisting of the culm inside the sheath. Sometimes in large grasses, particularly in sugar-cane and in bamboos, the leaves fall, leaving the culm naked. In relatively few grasses the edges of the sheath are grown together, forming a tube. Sometimes the blade of the leaf is not developed. This is always the case in the leaves or scales of rhizomes (Fig. 9), and often in those of stolons and in the lowermost leaves of a culm, especially in bamboos. Blades may be flat or folded (often called conduplicate) or involute; that is, rolled lengthwise. Rarely the inrolled edges are grown together, so that the blade really has no upper surface. Such leaves are called terete (meaning rounded). Blades vary greatly in size, shape, and texture, smoothness or hairiness. In broad leaves there is sometimes a narrow neck, or **petiole** (leaf-stalk), between the sheath and the blade.

SUMMARY

Grasses are distinguished by jointed, round or flattened, usually hollow, culms, with solid nodes; 2-ranked leaves, composed of sheath and blade, with a ligule at their junction; and by the spikelets with 2-ranked glumes and florets.

REVIEW

(1) How is a grass distinguished from all other plants?

(2) Break a cornstalk and note the arrangement of the torn fibers standing out of the pith. Compare this with the cut end of any twig of a tree or shrub. Cut across a wheat, oat, or rye straw and compare with the cornstalk and with the twig.

(3) Examine the culm (nodes and internodes) above and below ground and leaves (sheath, ligule, and blade) of any available grass.

(4) How is a rhizome distinguished from a root?

(5) What is the difference between a rhizome and a stolon?

LESSON II

THE SPIKELET AND THE INFLORESCENCE

Theoretically the spikelet is a reduced leafy branch. In the generalized spikelet shown in Fig. 8 the likeness to a jointed culm with 2-ranked leaves (Fig. 1) is readily seen, the glumes and lemmas corresponding to sheaths, their blades not developed. The palea, with two nerves and with its back to the axis, corresponds to a minute bract (the prophyllum) borne at the base of a branch in the axil of a sheath. The prophyllum is always 2-nerved, with its back (that is, the space between the nerves) against the main axis and its margins clasping the young branch. The flower, also, is theoretically an ultimate branchlet. In the flower-bearing lemmas, therefore, the palea is developed, while in the glumes, bearing no flowers, there are no paleas. Glumes and lemmas are, morphologically, reduced leaves, the lower pair, not flower-bearing, being termed **glumes,** the flower-bearing ones being termed **lemmas.** (See Fig. 7.)

The jointed axis of the spikelet (the rachilla) corresponds to the jointed culm and, like it, usually breaks at the nodes, the internode (the part of the rachilla between two nodes) remaining attached to the floret at its base (Fig. 4), just as in a broken grass stem the internode of the culm remains with the sheath that surrounds it; that is, the break normally comes just under the node. Rachis (which means the spine, or backbone) and axis (the imaginary central line of any body) are often used interchangeably as botanical terms. In most recent works on grasses and in these lessons, **axis** is used for the main axis of a compound inflorescence, **rachis** for the axis or support of the spikelets. In Fig. 10 are shown the axis of a panicle (A) and the rachis of a raceme (B); the rachis of the spike (C) is concealed by the overlapping spikelets.

FIG. 10. Forms of inflorescence: A, panicle; B, raceme; C, spike.

Spikelets are borne **pediceled** (that is, on a pedicel or foot stalk) or **sessile** (without a pedicel) in leafless panicles, racemes, or spikes (Fig. 10). These different types of inflorescence insensibly grade into each other. The axis and branches of a panicle and the rachis of a raceme or spike may be as elaborately modified and specialized as may be the parts of a spikelet. The axis, rachis, or branches may be **continuous** (not jointed), or **articulate** (jointed) and usually disarticulating (breaking up). The breaking up takes place at definite points and has to do with scattering the seed. The point of disarticulation is the same in grasses of the same kind (or genus) and is usually alike in related genera, and for this reason is of great importance in the classification of grasses. When there are no joints in the axis or branches, the disarticulation comes in the spikelet, either above the glumes and between the florets or below the glumes. Modifications of these two ways of disarticulating will be met with later. The study of the form of inflorescence and the modification of its parts will be carried on together with that of the spikelet.

SUMMARY

A spikelet consists of glumes and florets, in two ranks and alternate on the rachilla, the florets consisting of lemma, palea, and the inclosed flower. Every organ found in the most highly specialized spikelet is to be interpreted as an elaboration or a reduction of one of these parts. The spikelet is the unit of the inflorescence; the floret is the unit of the spikelet. The spikelet is always simple; that is, the rachilla never branches. The floret is always 1-flowered with never more than one lemma and one palea; the glumes and florets are always alternate, two consecutive ones never being borne one above the other.

These basic facts kept in mind will aid in the recognition of complicated or congested spikelets and in the correct interpretation of their parts.

REVIEW

(1) Examine a spikelet of a brome-grass, such as cheat or chess. Separate the florets from each other and from the glumes. Note that these disjoint without tearing. Open out the lemma and palea. Note that these permanently adhere at their base; that they can only be torn or cut apart.

(2) Name the parts of a spikelet.

(3) What is their arrangement?

(4) What is the difference between a rachis and a rachilla?

LESSON III

MODIFICATIONS OF THE SPIKELET

Taking the generalized spikelet as a beginning, examine Figs. 4 and 8. Note that the glumes and lemmas have nerves or veins (fibro-vascular bundles) running from the base to the apex or nearly to it, one nerve in the middle and an equal number on each side, there being an odd number of nerves in the glumes and lemmas. In the palea there are only two nerves; none in the middle. The modifications and variations of spikelets will be studied, as nearly as possible, in the order of their increasing complexity. No attempt should be made to fix in mind the forms of specialization here enumerated. This lesson is only meant to put one on the lookout for modifications, so that one may be prepared to recognize a given organ under various guises.

(1) Spikelets differ in size. (Bromus or brome-grass, meadow fescue, and blue-grass are examples.)

(2) The number of florets may be reduced to one or increased to twenty or more.

(3) The parts of the spikelet vary in their relative sizes. The glumes may be large and the florets small or the florets large and the glumes small.

(4) The rachilla joints may be slender or thick, so short that the florets appear to be opposite, or nearly

as long as the florets themselves; the node at the base of the floret (the **callus**) is sometimes prolonged into a sharp point; the uppermost rachilla joint may bear no floret and may extend into a little bristle.

(5) The glumes may vary in shape, in texture, and in the number of their nerves and may be glabrous (smooth) or pubescent (hairy); sometimes they are reduced to rudiments and sometimes they are suppressed.

(6) The lemma is subject to such great modifications that we shall now note only the simplest ones. As in the glumes, the shape and texture and the number of nerves vary. The summit of the lemma may be acute (pointed) or acuminate (long-pointed) or obtuse (blunt) or it may be lobed or cleft. The nerves may be faint or strong, or may extend into **awns** (bristles) beyond the body of the lemma. The lemma is sometimes minute, but it is never suppressed.

(7) The palea is always 2-nerved, but in a few grasses the nerves are so close together as to appear like a single one. In others they are far apart and the palea may split between them. The palea differs in size and texture. In a few genera it is reduced or even suppressed.

(8) Spikelets are compressed (flattened) laterally (sidewise), as in Figs. 11–14, or dorsally (on the back), as in Figs. 60–66. The side or back of a spikelet is recognized from the position of the florets on the rachilla. The palea side of the floret is always

toward the rachilla. Taking this as the "front" of a floret, the back (or dorsum) is the back of the lemma. Spikelets with many florets, or those in which the glumes or lemmas are folded on the mid-nerve, are generally laterally compressed; those with a single fertile floret and with convex (rounded) glumes and lemma are generally dorsally compressed.

(9) Spikelets are sometimes **unisexual** (of one sex) instead of **perfect** (having both stamens and pistil). The two kinds, **pistillate** (the ovule-producing) and **staminate** (pollen-producing) may be borne on a single plant, as in corn, with pistillate spikelets in the ear and staminate spikelets in the tassel, or in different plants, as in salt-grass and buffalo-grass. Grasses with staminate and pistillate spikelets on the same plants are **monœcious** (which means dwelling in one house); those with staminate and pistillate spikelets on different plants are **diœcious** (dwelling in two houses). The unisexual spikelets of a single species may be similar in appearance, or they may be very unlike, as in corn.

(10) Some grasses with perfect spikelets bear in addition staminate spikelets or **neuter** spikelets (having neither stamens nor pistils). These additional spikelets may be similar in appearance to the perfect ones or very unlike them. They are borne in the same inflorescence as the perfect spikelets and are usually paired with them.

(11) The florets of a single spikelet may be of two kinds, perfect and sterile, the sterile being either

staminate or neuter. In spikelets like those of Figs. 11–14, with several to many florets, the uppermost florets are commonly sterile (not perfecting seed), though they are like the fertile florets in appearance and have rudimentary stamens and pistils. In some grasses the sterile florets are very different from the fertile ones and may be borne above or below them on the rachilla. The position of sterile florets in the spikelet is the same in large series of related grasses; hence it is of great importance in classifying genera. The type of modification of the sterile floret is also uniform within a genus, and generally in related genera. It commonly consists of a lemma without a palea, but there may be a rudimentary or even a well-developed palea.

These types of modification will be brought out and illustrated in the succeeding lessons.

SUMMARY

All spikelets are built on the simple plan of 2-ranked florets with a pair of glumes at the base. The spikelet as a whole and each of its organs is subject to modification. The palea and one or both glumes may be suppressed; the lemma may be reduced but is never suppressed. The position and type of modification of sterile florets are of importance in classification.

The parts of a spikelet, however complex, are recognizable as rachilla, glumes, lemma, or palea.

LESSON IV

PEDICELED SPIKELETS OF FEW TO MANY FLORETS

TAKING the spikelet of cheat or chess (*Bromus secalinus*), Fig. 11, as a starting point, we have one but little different from the diagrammatic spikelet (Fig. 8). [Names incidentally mentioned should not be memorized.] The lemmas are convex on the back, several-nerved, 2-toothed at the apex and bear an awn from between the teeth. The awn is the midnerve extending beyond the body of the lemma. The rachilla joints are short, bringing the florets (Fig. 11, B) close together. The articulation is above the glumes and between the florets. The palea is grown fast to the grain. All species of Bromus have spikelets of this character, differing in size, texture, length of the awn, which may be much longer or reduced to a mucro (a minute point) or even suppressed, in being glabrous, as in cheat, or pubescent. The pubescence may cover the lemma

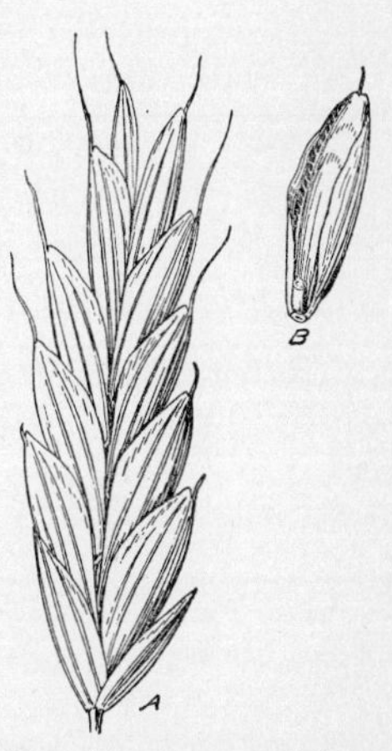

FIG. 11. A, several-flowered spikelet of *Bromus secalinus*; B, single floret.

9129

or be along the margins only. These differences distinguish the species. A genus is composed of one to many species having few to several important characters in common, and presumably descended from a common ancestor. Groups of species having less important characters in common form related genera. Festuca (Fig. 12) is related to Bromus, having few to several-flowered spikelets, disarticulating above the glumes and between the florets and with several-nerved lemmas; but the lemmas are awned from the tip, or pointed only, and not toothed, and the palea is not grown to the grain.

FIG. 12. A, spikelet of *Festuca ovina;* B, lemma detached.

A large number of grasses have laterally compressed spikelets of this general type, disarticulating above the glumes and between the few to many florets. They are sorted into genera and the genera separated from each other chiefly according to the modifications of the lemma. In Panicularia (Fig. 13) the lemmas are broad and obtuse with strong parallel nerves. In Poa (Fig. 14) the lemmas are keeled on the back and have five nerves converging toward the acute but never awned apex. The species figured (Kentucky blue-grass, *Poa pratensis*) and many others are villous (having soft curly hairs) on the lower part of the midnerve and the marginal nerves and have a tuft of white cottony hairs at the base, but this pubescence is not found in all the species.

In all the grasses mentioned so far, the spikelets are borne in panicles (see Fig. 10, A). Spikelets much like those of Panicularia (Fig. 13) but borne in a raceme and having awned lemmas are found in Pleuropogon (shown in Fig. 10, B). In these spikelets the palea is crested or winged on the nerves (Fig. 15, showing a three quarter view of a palea removed from the floret).

FIG. 14. Spikelet of *Poa pratensis.*

FIG. 13. Spikelet of *Panicularia septentrionalis.*

Returning to Fig. 11, A, we note the midnerve of the lemma extending as an awn beyond the minutely toothed apex. The midnerve and the two lateral nerves as well are extended into awns in *Triodia flava* (Fig. 16, the floret seen from the back); the apex of the lemma is toothed and the nerves are villous below. In Fig. 17 (floret of *Cottea pappophoroides* opened out and seen from the back) the lemma is lobed and nine to eleven of its many nerves are extended into awns.

FIG. 15. Palea of *Pleuropogon californicus.*

After the foregoing the spikelet and its parts will be recognized in most of the genera of the group having few to many-flowered pediceled spikelets. As stated in Lesson III the florets in a single spikelet may be of two kinds. The simplest spikelet of this type is found in the reed (*Phragmites communis*). In this, the lowest floret is staminate or neuter and its lemma is much longer than in the other florets (Fig. 18, A). In the perfect floret (Fig. 18, B) it will be seen that the palea is very much shorter than the lemma, that the

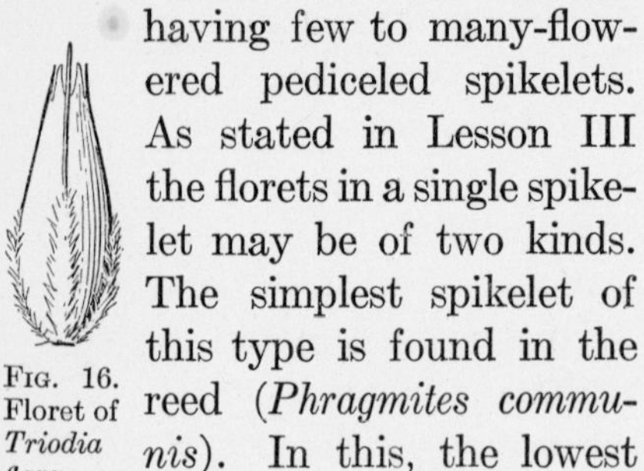

Fig. 16. Floret of *Triodia flava.*

Fig. 17. Lemma of *Cottea pappophoroides.*

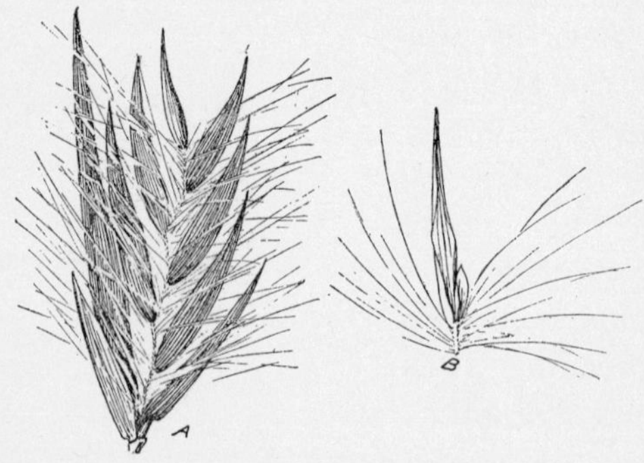

Fig. 18. A, spikelet of *Phragmites communis*; B, floret.

rachilla bears copious long soft hairs, and that instead of disarticulating at its summit and remaining attached to the floret next below, it disarticulates at its base, remaining as a tiny feathery stem to the floret next above, its copious long hairs carrying the floret before the wind, dispersing the seed. [The hairs are much more copious than shown in the figure; they are slighted to avoid obscuring the difference in the florets.]

FIG. 19. Spikelet of *Melica mutica.*

Another spikelet with two kinds of florets is shown in Fig. 19 (*Melica mutica*). In this the lemmas of the upper florets are reduced in size, changed in shape, and contain no flower. Two or three of them are crowded together in a little club-shaped body. In the species figured, this modification is more marked than in most of the species.

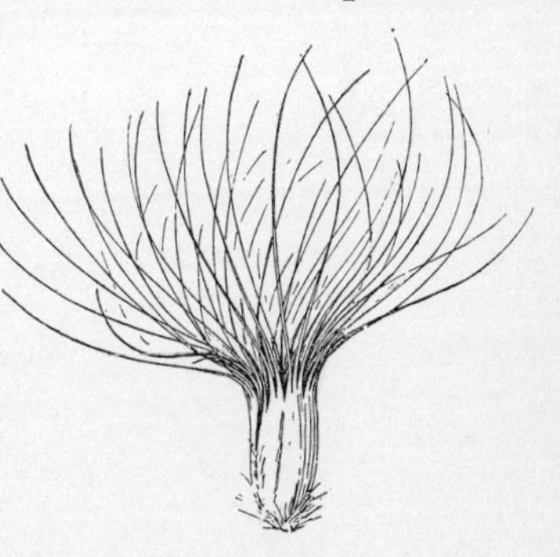

FIG. 20. Florets of *Pappophorum vaginatum.*

In Fig. 20 is shown a side view of the florets of a spikelet of *Pappophorum vaginatum*, the glumes removed. The lowest floret is perfect. Its broad lemma is cut into many spreading awns (compare with Fig. 17). The two to four other florets are crowded on the very short rachilla and are sterile; their lemmas are similar to that of the one fertile floret. The rachilla does not disarticulate, the sterile florets remaining permanently attached to the fertile one, the numerous awns of all together forming a pappus-like crown which carries the seed before the wind. [Pappus is the "down" on the seed of a dandelion, thistle, or other plant of their family.]

Next we shall examine the inflorescence of a grass having spikelets entirely of sterile florets in addition to spikelets of fertile florets. Examine Fig. 21, A (*Cynosurus cristatus*), which shows a small part of a spike-like panicle. The spikelets are borne on minute pedicels on very short compound branches. The lower one to three spikelets of each little branch are sterile, the lemmas containing no flowers (Fig. 21, B). The upper one to three spikelets are smaller and fertile (Fig. 21, C). When the bracts of the sterile spikelet are all alike empty, why are all but the lower pair called lemmas, instead of glumes? In many cases the nature of modified organs can only be recognized by their correspondence to organs in the same relative position in allied but more simple forms. In all the spikelets examined

FIG. 21. A, part of a panicle of *Cynosurus cristatus;* B, sterile spikelet; C, fertile spikelet.

so far (and in all but a very small number of grasses) the bracts above the lower pair are flower-bearing or have a palea, which indicates their structural identity. Corresponding parts in a modified spikelet are, therefore, regarded as lemmas. In the grass just examined the sterile spikelets remain on the panicle branches after the fall of the ripened fertile florets from their glumes.

In Fig. 22, A (*Achyrodes aureum*), is shown a fascicle of one fertile and three sterile spikelets of another grass. In this the fascicles hang from the short slender branches of a narrow panicle and disarticulate from them, falling entire. This is the first example we have had so far of disarticulating branches of the inflorescence. In the figure the fascicle is seen from the inner face to show the fertile spikelet, which from the outside is nearly hidden by the sterile ones. Fig. 22, B, shows a separate fertile spikelet. It will be seen that except for the glumes, the two forms are strikingly different. The fertile spikelet is reduced to one fertile and one rudimentary floret, both awned,

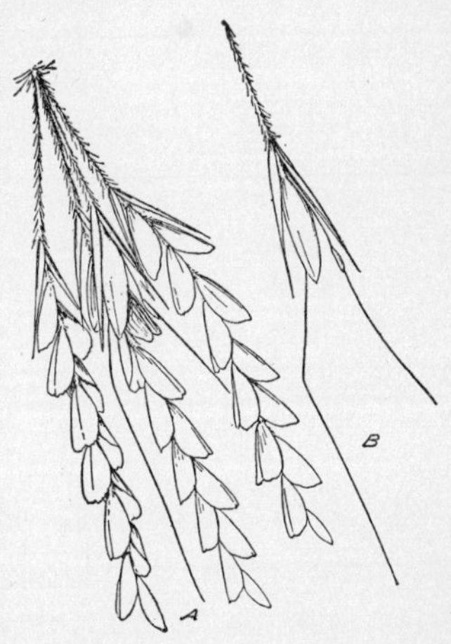

Fig. 22. A, fascicle of three sterile and one fertile spikelet of *Achyrodes aureum;* B, fertile spikelet.

while the sterile spikelets are many-flowered and awnless.

We shall next examine a grass having unisexual spikelets (see Lesson III, page 23), the two forms borne on different plants (diœcious). (In the group with relatively simple spikelets which we are now studying there are no monœcious grasses). In Fig. 23 are shown the pistillate and staminate spikelets of salt-grass (*Distichlis spicata*). They differ but little in appearance and are both

Fig. 23. Pistillate and staminate spikelets of *Distichlis spicata.*

borne in narrow panicles. [♀ signifies female, ♂ male. These signs are commonly used to indicate pistillate and staminate plants, respectively.]

In Fig. 24 are seen the strikingly diverse staminate and pistillate spikelets of another diœcious species

Fig. 24. Staminate and pistillate spikelets of *Scleropogon brevifolius.*

(*Scleropogon brevifolius*). The lemmas of the staminate spikelet are merely pointed; those of the pistillate spikelet bear three long slender twisted spreading awns. The pistillate florets fall from the glumes as a whole (the rachilla not disarticulating between them) and roll before the wind as tiny tumble weeds.

SUMMARY

The inflorescence and the two to several-flowered spikelets of the brome-grasses, blue-grasses and their relatives are comparatively simple. In a few genera sterile spikelets are developed and in a few others the spikelets are unisexual.

REVIEW

Collect specimens of orchard-grass, meadow fescue, any species of brome-grass, or of Poa, or of any available grasses having laterally compressed, few to several-flowered spikelets. Identify the different parts of the spikelets. Lemmas may be spread out for examination by cutting off the very base with a sharp knife or scalpel. Spikelets of tough or rigid texture if soaked in water for a few minutes may be dissected without tearing. If very tough or hard, boiling the spikelets in water with a little glycerine (a drop of glycerine to about a teaspoonful of water) will make them manageable and keep them from drying out during dissection.

LESSON V

SESSILE SPIKELETS IN TWO-SIDED SPIKES

RETURNING again to the spikelet of *Bromus secalinus* (Fig. 11), we shall strike out in another direction. Differentiation among living beings does not follow a line, but radiates like waves following the falling of a pebble in the water, or rather like waves of sound, in all directions. Hence we can not follow an unbroken line in studying the increasing complexity of the inflorescence of grasses. We can only return to the center and start out on another line. Compare Fig. 10, A and B, with C, and with Fig. 25 (couch-grass or quack-grass, *Agropyron repens*). A raceme is a panicle reduced to its lowest terms. Eliminating the pedicels of the spikelets of a raceme we have a spike, the spikelets set directly upon the rachis. In such an inflorescence the rachis is usually more or less thickened. In Fig. 25, A, part of a spike is shown from the flat side of the spikelet. The rachis is jointed and a spikelet is

FIG. 25. A, part of a spike of *Agropyron repens*; B, part of rachis seen from the edge, all but two spikelets removed.

borne at each joint, alternating on opposite sides. The rachis is thickened and the joints slightly hollowed on alternate sides. (See Fig. 25, B, a diagrammatic illustration of the rachis seen from the edge with all but two spikelets removed.)

The spikelet is not very different from that of Bromus (Fig. 11) and as in that, the ripened florets fall from the glumes.

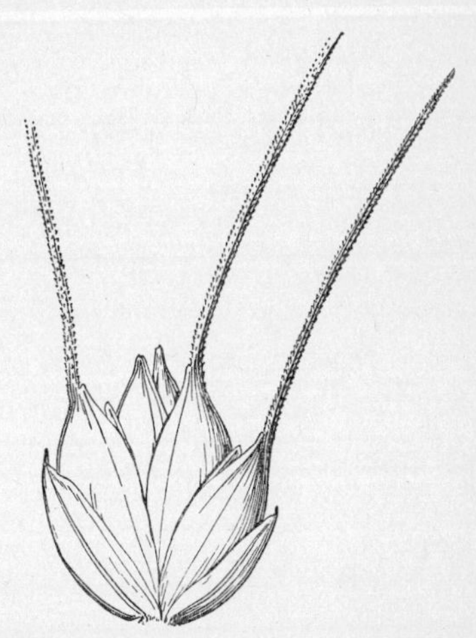
Fig. 26. Spikelet of *Triticum æstivum.*

In the group of grasses taken up in this lesson the specialization is mostly in the rachis and in the position of the relatively simple spikelets.

In Fig. 26, a spikelet of cultivated wheat (*Triticum æstivum*), we have the same type of spikelet as in Fig. 25 but with fewer and much plumper florets, with broader lemmas slightly toothed at the apex, and with long awns that are scabrous (rough, like a file). [Awns form the "beard" of wheat.] The spikelets are borne on a jointed rachis as in Fig. 25 (*Agropyron repens*) but the joints are shorter, bringing the spikelets closer together and hiding the rachis. In this, cultivated wheat, the florets do not readily fall from the glumes but remain in the spike and the ripened grain is thrashed from them. This persistence of the lemma and palea has been fixed by selection in cultivation. In the closely related emmer (*Triticum dicoccum*) the rachis breaks at the joints, each joint remaining attached to its spikelet.

Fig. 27. Part of a spike of *Lolium multiflorum*.

Compare Fig. 27 (*Lolium multiflorum*) with Fig. 25. Note that in Fig. 25 the spikelets are borne flat side against the rachis, while in Fig. 27 they stand with their edges against the rachis. The rachis itself is of the same type as that in Fig. 25. The diagrammatic rachis with two spikelets seen edgewise (Fig. 25, B) is shown from the same position as is Fig. 27. In this, as in Agropyron, the rachis is continuous (not disarticulating) and the florets fall. If we separate a spikelet from the rachis we find that the first glume (the one that would be against the rachis) is suppressed, the first floret lying directly against the rachis. In the single spikelet borne at the summit of the rachis the first glume is developed and is about as large as the second. When but one glume is present, we know which glume it is and which is suppressed by the position of the first floret, which is always above the first glume. When no glume is found below the first floret, it is obvious that it is the first glume which is suppressed.

In Fig. 28 (*Lepturus cylindricus*) we have a greatly thickened, strongly nerved rachis with spikelets placed as in Fig. 27 but reduced to the second glume and a single floret. This little spikelet is sunken in the hollow of the rachis joint, the second glume fitting snugly over the hollow, the whole forming a long, slender, wiry cylinder. At maturity the rachis disarticulates with the spikelets firmly embedded in the joints. (See diagram of rachis, Fig. 28, B, and, above, a joint with spikelet removed, showing the hollow, and a second with the spikelet in position.) The plant bearing these spikes grows along mud flats near the sea. The rachis joints are cylindrical and readily roll down the slope to the water. Being corky, they are carried by the lightest ripples and are thus spread over wide areas. The grain germinates within its little cell, and the young roots and leaves push aside the water-soaked glume.

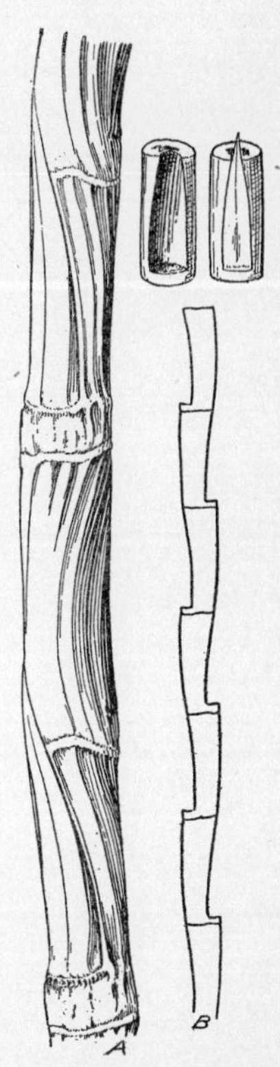

FIG. 28. A, part of spike of *Lepturus cylindricus*; B, diagram of rachis, spikelets removed; above, diagram of single joint.

Returning to Fig. 25 with its one spikelet at each joint, flat against the rachis, compare with it Fig. 29 (*Elymus virginicus*, or rye-grass). In this there are two spikelets at each joint of the rachis, the first glumes back to back, the spikelets somewhat distorted, each pair reaching around the edges of the rachis. The figure shows a pair of spikelets and two joints of the rachis, with the pair of spikelets next above, on the opposite side of the rachis, lightly sketched in behind; two more internodes of the rachis, with spikelets removed, are shown by dotted lines. A diagrammatic sketch of a pair of spikelets, the distortion reduced, is shown above. A comparison of the diagrammatic spikelet with the spikelet in Fig. 25 will show the structural similarity. In their natural position the spikelets,

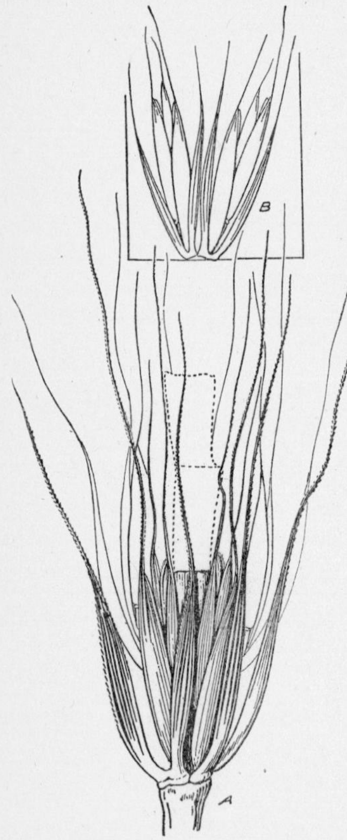

FIG. 29. A, pair of spikelets of *Elymus virginicus*; B, diagrammatic figure of the pair of spikelets.

overlapping on the short joints and extending around the edges of the rachis, so that at least one is seen nearly edge-wise, form a spike that may well be confusing to the beginner, especially when, as in the species shown in Fig. 29 and several others, the glumes stand out like a 4-rayed involucre below the appressed florets. However, a single joint with its spikelets attached cut out of the spike readily discloses the structure. In some species of Elymus there are three spikelets and occasionally four or five at a node, the distortion being correspondingly greater. In several species the glumes are so narrow as to appear like bristles or awns only. In most of the species the rachis is continuous and can not be disjointed. In a closely related genus, Sitanion, the rachis disarticulates at the base of each joint, the slender rigid joint remaining as a tiny sharp-pointed stem below the cluster of long-awned spikelets. The awn-like glumes of Sitanion commonly split between the nerves, sometimes to the very base, appearing like a cluster of awns below the florets.

In Elymus and Sitanion the spikelets are all alike (or some occasionally variously aborted) and all sessile (set directly on the rachis). In Fig. 30 (*Hordeum nodosum*, one of the wild barleys), a group of three spikelets and a joint of the rachis are shown. As in Sitanion the rachis disarticulates at the base of the internode, the joint remaining attached to the spikelets above it. Note that the central spikelet is sessile and the lateral ones pediceled, that the lower floret of the central spikelet is well developed while those of the lateral florets are rudimentary, and that the back of the floret is turned from the rachis with the glumes (bristle-like in this species) at the sides or back, contrary to the arrangement characteristic of grass spikelets. The problem of the glumes in Hordeum has not been satisfactorily solved. It appears probable that the reduced rachilla joint between the second glume and the floret is twisted and bent inward, bringing the glumes at the side or back of the floret. In the cultivated barley the rachis does not break up, as in the wild species, the continuous rachis having been fixed by selection. The florets fall from the spike in thrashing, or in naked or hull-less barley the grains fall from the lemma and palea, as in wheat. In cultivated 2-rowed barley the lateral spikelets are pediceled and sterile, as in the wild species, but in 4-rowed and 6-rowed barley the lateral spikelets are sessile and fertile, characters fixed by selection.

Fig. 30. Joint of spike of *Hordeum nodosum*.

The grasses characterized by the spicate inflorescence dealt with in this lesson form the barley tribe, which from the standpoint of man is the most important group of grasses, if not of all plants, in the world, containing wheat, barley, and rye.

SUMMARY

The specialization in spicate inflorescence is chiefly in the rachis and next in the position of the relatively simple spikelets.

When the glumes are distorted, standing side by side, as often found in species of Elymus, or when one of them is suppressed, we can tell which is which from the fact that the first, or lowermost, floret is always above or on the same side of the spikelet as the first glume.

REVIEW

Collect heads of wheat, rye, barley, quack-grass, species of Elymus, Lolium, or squirrel-tail grass (one or more of these will be found anywhere in the United States). Note whether the rachis readily disjoints. If so, separate out a single joint with the spikelets attached. Note where the rachis breaks, at the summit or base of the joint; note the number of spikelets at a joint and the number of florets to a spikelet. Distinguish the individual spikelets and their parts. If the rachis does not disjoint, cut across the middle of the internodes, taking out a single joint with attached spikelets. Note the number of spikelets to a joint; whether there are one or two to several fertile florets to the spikelet and whether the spikelet is placed flatwise or edgewise to the rachis.

Note how spikes bearing spikelets with scabrous awns push themselves forward when handled.

LESSON VI

PEDICELED SPIKELETS WITH LARGE GLUMES AND OTHER MODIFICATIONS

TURNING again to the spikelet of *Bromus secalinus* (Fig. 11), compare with it Fig. 31 (wild oats, *Avena fatua*). The glumes are greatly enlarged and the rachilla joints are so short that the florets appear to be almost opposite. The awn, instead of extending from the apex of the lemma, protrudes from the back and is twisted for about half its length. We noted in Lesson IV that the awn is an extension of the midnerve. This fact is well shown in the floret of wild oats (Fig. 31, B, the floret seen from the back), in

FIG. 31. A, spikelet of *Avena fatua;* B, floret.

which the midnerve leaves the body of the lemma about the middle of its back and becomes a free awn, while the lemma above the departure of the awn is nerveless. This is invariably the case when

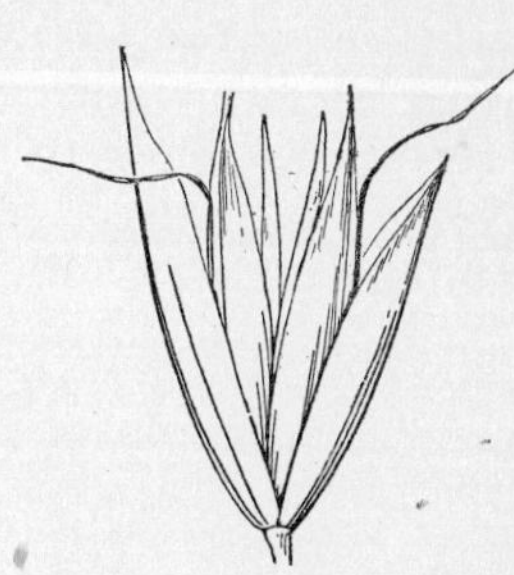

FIG. 32. Spikelet of *Trisetum spicatum.*

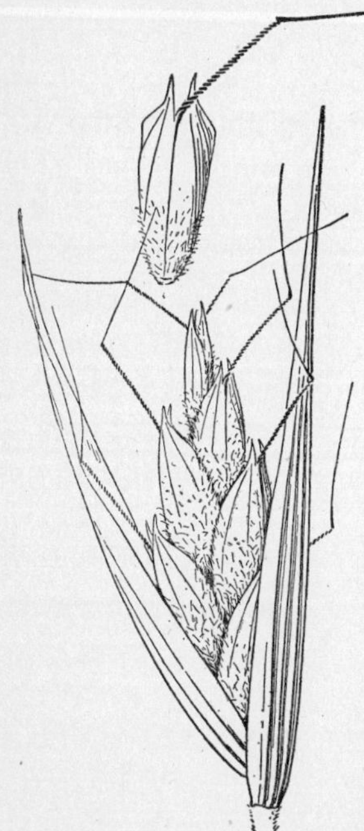

FIG. 33. Spikelet of *Danthonia spicata;* floret above.

the awn is dorsal (that is, protruding from the back); the lemma is always nerveless above it.

Compare Figs. 31 and 32 (*Trisetum spicatum*). It will be seen that they are the same type of spikelet. In Trisetum the awn is loosely twisted and is borne nearer the apex of the lemma, which is tipped with two slender teeth.

In *Danthonia spicata* (Fig. 33) the florets are more numerous and are smaller in proportion to the glumes. The broad strongly twisted awn arises from between the teeth or lobes of a bidentate (2-toothed) apex (see floret above, seen from the back).

In these three spikelets, as in all but a few of the grasses of the oat tribe, the florets fall from the glumes which remain on the pedicel. In velvet grass, *Notholcus lanatus* (Fig. 34), the spikelet falls entire. The articulation of the spikelet, taken throughout the grass family, is so nearly uniform for related genera that it is relied on to differentiate large series. (See Lesson II, on inflorescence). There are exceptions to the mode of articulation characteristic of the group as a whole in the case of a few genera in three of our tribes. Such exceptions are puzzling to the beginner, leading him astray in using keys. We must learn to observe *all* the characters of the inflorescence and base our judgment on the *sum total* of the characters, remembering that "Nature does as she pleases" and rejoicing that in grasses she at least pleases to keep invariably to the 2-ranked arrangement of the spikelets. (See the summary of Lesson II). In Lesson IV, Figs. 18 and 19, we observed spikelets in which the florets were of two kinds. In *Notholcus lanatus* the lower floret is perfect and awnless and the upper is staminate and bears a hook-like awn from the back (Fig. 34, B,

FIG. 34. A, spikelet of *Notholeus lanatus;* B, pair of florets.

florets removed from the glumes. Note the curved and exceptionally long lowermost rachilla joint.)

In Sphenopholis, closely related to Trisetum (Fig. 32), the spikelets fall entire, as in velvet-grass. In tall oat-grass (*Arrhenatherum elatius*) the spikelets bear one perfect awnless floret and one staminate awned floret, as in velvet-grass, but their position is reversed, the staminate being below and the perfect above.

SUMMARY

In the oat and its relatives the large glumes and the awn of the lemmas are the most prominent characters, although in species of some genera the awn is wanting. Pubescence is commonly conspicuous. The inflorescence is an open or contracted panicle.

REVIEW

Collect panicles of wild oats or awned specimens of cultivated oats (cultivated oats growing wild commonly bear awns), of Danthonia, one or more species of which are to be found throughout most of the United States, and any of the related grasses available, and examine the spikelets. Place a floret with a twisted awn in a drop of water and observe the result. In awnless florets of cultivated oats note that the midnerve of the lemma, if it is not at all produced into an awn, stops abruptly at the point where the awn would arise normally and that the lemma is nerveless above this point, just as if it were awned.

LESSON VII

PEDICELED ONE-FLOWERED SPIKELETS

TURN to the spikelet of wild oats (Fig. 31) and in imagination eliminate all but the lowest floret and the glumes. Better still, with a spikelet of oats in hand break off all above the lowest floret. Now we have a large model or pattern of the reduced spikelet of a very large number of grasses, red-top, timothy, and their kind.

Examine *Calamagrostis canadensis* (Fig. 35, the floret raised from its glumes) and note how it corresponds to the pattern obtained by reducing the spikelet of oats to a single floret. The only vestige remaining of the other florets is the minute rachilla joint back of the palea (shown, exaggerated somewhat, in Fig. 35). In all but a few genera the rachilla is entirely suppressed. Compare Fig. 35 with Fig. 32 and note that Trisetum reduced to a single floret would closely resemble Calamagrostis.

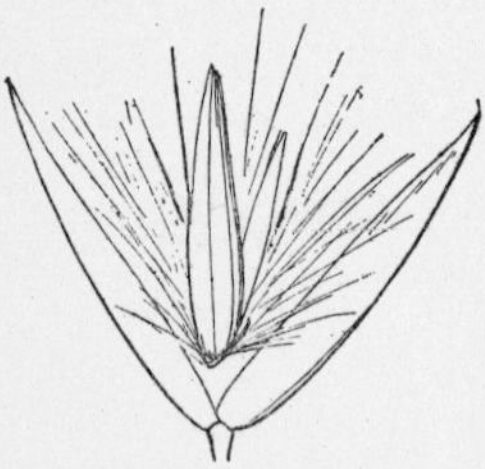

FIG. 35. Spikelet of *Calamagrostis canadensis.*

In Agrostis (Fig. 36) the rachilla is normally suppressed. In two species in the far West it is present as a minute rudiment. In most of the species the palea also is suppressed or represented by a rudiment only (Fig. 36, *Agrostis hiemalis*, the floret with palea wanting, raised from the glumes). Here we have specialization through elimination, the spikelet reduced almost to its lowest terms, one floret with no palea, no awn, no callus hairs. In this particular species the very open panicles break off and roll before the wind as tumbleweeds, scattering the seed. Several species of Agrostis have awned lemmas and some have callus hairs, shorter and less copious than in Calamagrostis.

FIG. 36. Spikelet of *Agrostis hiemalis*.

In Sporobolus (Fig. 37, the floret raised from the glumes and containing a mature grain) the nerves of the palea are wide apart and the internerve (the space between the nerves) is thin in texture and readily splits as the grain matures. In some species it splits to the apex, resulting in an object sorely puzzling to the beginner, the two halves appearing like two 1-nerved lemmas or paleas, in addition to the lemma itself. It is in such cases as this that a knowledge of the structure of the grass spikelet is necessary for the correct interpretation of the organs observed. In this genus and in a few others the **pericarp** (meaning around the fruit), the wall of the ripened ovary which forms a covering

FIG. 37. Spikelet of *Sporobolus airoides*.

for the grain and is usually grown fast to it, is free from the grain. In most of the species it is a loose thin sac, which readily tears when moistened, leaving the grain naked. In one of our species (*Sporobolus heterolepis*) the pericarp is firm, like a thin shell about the grain.

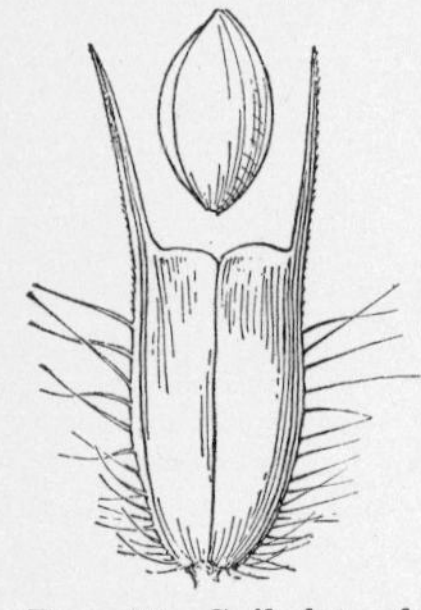

Fig. 38. Spikelet of *Phleum pratense;* floret above.

In Cinna the two nerves of the palea are so close together that they appear to be a single nerve. In one of the species this nerve may be easily split into two, demonstrating the derivation of the apparent single nerve.

In several genera the glumes are enlarged. In timothy (Fig. 38) they are firm in texture, strongly keeled, and abruptly awned, while the lemma is much smaller, thin in texture, and awnless. The spikelets are so congested on the short branches of the cylindrical spike-like panicle that the beginner may be puzzled to know just what is the unit of inflorescence. Keeping in mind that a spikelet never is compound, the student will divide and redivide the cluster until he finds an object having a single pair of glumes containing the floret.

Fig. 39. Spikelet of *Alopecurus geniculatus.*

Another modification of the glumes

is shown in Alopecurus (Fig. 39). The margins are grown together for half their length. As in *Notholcus lanatus* (Fig. 34) the articulation is an exception to that generally characteristic of its allied genera, the spikelets falling entire. The lemma bears a delicate dorsal awn and the palea is suppressed. In most species of Alopecurus the panicle is as dense and spike-like as that of timothy.

In some genera the glumes are reduced (see Fig. 42), and in a few species the first glume is suppressed.

In Lesson IV, Fig. 21, we noted perfect and sterile spikelets in the same panicle and in Fig. 22 we found the spikelets falling in clusters of three sterile and one perfect spikelet. In Lycurus (Fig. 40) the spikelets are in pairs on the ultimate branchlets of the spike-like panicle, the lower spikelet sterile, the upper perfect. The ultimate branchlet itself falls with the spikelets attached, as in Achyrodes (Fig. 22). Lycurus shows another peculiar character in the 2-nerved first glume, one lateral nerve being undeveloped or very faint. The midnerve is extended into a long awn and the one lateral nerve is usually extended into a shorter awn, but is sometimes a mere tooth.

Fig. 40. Pair of spikelets, sterile and fertile (spread apart) of *Lycurus phleoides*.

The glumes and lemma in the spikelets so far examined in this lesson have been of like texture, membranaceous (like a membrane or skin).

In Muhlenbergia (Figs. 41 and 42) the lemma is firmer in texture than the glumes. In some species of the genus the glumes are much reduced, and in some they are well developed and often awned. The lemmas are prominently 3-nerved and are awned or mucronate, that is, the midnerve extending in a minute point.

Fig. 41. Spikelet of *Muhlenbergia foliosa.*

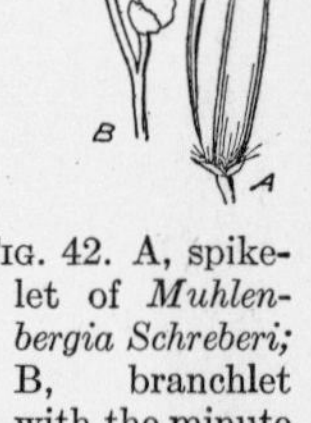

Fig. 42. A, spikelet of *Muhlenbergia Schreberi;* B, branchlet with the minute glumes of two spikelets from which florets have fallen.

In four of our genera the lemma at maturity is firm and hard in texture and the nerves are scarcely visible. In Milium (Fig. 43) the lemma is rigid, smooth, and shining and the palea is of like texture. In Oryzopsis (Fig. 44) the lemma bears an awn that readily disarticulates at its base. The palea is nearly inclosed by the lemma.

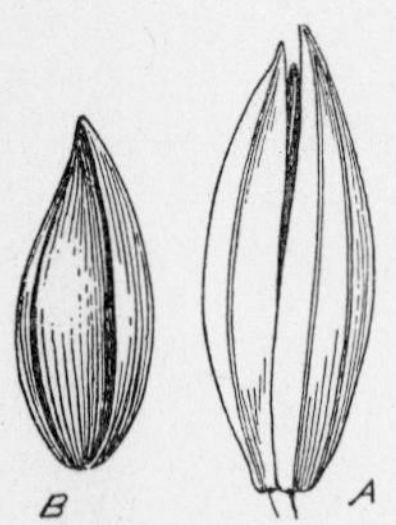

Fig. 43. A, spikelet of *Milium effusum;* B, floret.

In Stipa (Fig. 45) and Aristida (Fig. 46) the palea is entirely inclosed in the lemma. The callus (see

FIG. 44. A, glumes, and B, floret of *Oryzopsis racemosa.*

FIG. 45. A, glumes, and B, floret of *Stipa spartea.*

FIG. 46. Spikelet of *Aristida dichotoma.*

page 22) is developed into a needle-like point that readily penetrates clothing or works its way into the wool of sheep.

In Stipa the awn is composed of all the nerves of the lemma, forming a solid slightly flattened elongate body, the point of departure from the body of the lemma being marked by an abrupt contraction or a ring of hairs. In some species the lower part of the awn is plumose (covered with soft fluffy hairs, like a feather).

In Aristida the awn is divided into three; that is, the three nerves at first unite, then separate. The lemma tapers into the awn with no visible junction, as in Stipa. Sometimes the undivided part of the awn is elongate, forming a slender neck and sometimes this neck is twisted. In *Aristida dichotoma*, the species shown (Fig. 46), the lateral awns are much shorter than the central one. In many species the three are subequal, and one or all may be recurved or loosely twisted at the base. They are never tightly twisted, as in Stipa.

SUMMARY

The specialization in this group of grasses consists in the reduction of the relatively simplified spikelet to a single floret. In most of the genera the spikelets are very small. The glumes may be reduced to rudiments or suppressed or may be well developed and somewhat elaborated. The lemma may be delicate or indurate (hardened) and may be awned from the back or the summit. The palea shows more modification in this group than in any other. It may be suppressed or it may be as long as the lemma; the two nerves may be coherent, appearing as one, or widely separated with the delicate internerve splitting. The rachilla may be extended beyond the base of the palea, a vestige of the suppressed florets, or it may be produced into a sharp callus below the lemma. The inflorescence is always a panicle, but this may be diffuse or dense and cylindrical or capitate (like a head).

REVIEW

Collect panicles of redtop, timothy, or of any grass with laterally compressed 1-flowered spikelets. If the inflorescence is dense, distinguish the individual spikelets. Dissect the spikelets and note whether any of the organs are suppressed. Note the point of attachment of the awn, if any.

If possible, collect panicles of any species of Stipa. Lay a few of the florets in a little water and note the result. Note that twisted awns or the twisted parts of an awn are flattened.

LESSON VIII

SESSILE SPIKELETS IN ONE-SIDED SPIKES

As stated in Lesson V, development does not follow a single line, so, having come to the end of one line, we must repeatedly return to the center and start in a new direction. In the group of grasses taken up in this lesson the principal character common to all is the spicate inflorescence. In the grasses related to barley (Lesson V) we found solitary 2-sided spikes, the spikelets sessile on opposite sides of the rachis. In the present group we have 1-sided (unilateral) spikes, the spikelets sessile or nearly so along one side of the rachis. The spikelets themselves range from the simple one of yard-grass, *Eleusine indica* (Fig. 47), to highly specialized ones. Compare Fig. 47, A, with Figs. 11 and 14. It will be seen that, although the glumes and lemmas of Eleusine are strongly keeled, the spikelets are of the same type; but these spikelets are very differently arranged (Fig. 47, B), being crowded and imbricate (overlapping like shingles) in two rows on one side of the rachis. Two to several of these spikes are borne together, digitate or nearly so. [Digitate means arranged like fingers (digits), but as a botanical term it indicates an arrangement more like that

Fig. 47. A, spikelet of *Eleusine indica;* B, inflorescence.

of a bird's toes, the spikes borne on so short an axis that they appear to spring from the same point.]

In Lesson VII we obtained the pattern of the 1-flowered spikelet by eliminating all but the lowest floret and the glumes from a several-flowered spikelet. Eliminating all but the lowest floret of Eleusine we have a model of the spikelet of Bermuda-grass, *Capriola Dactylon* (Fig. 48, A). A vestige of the eliminated florets re-

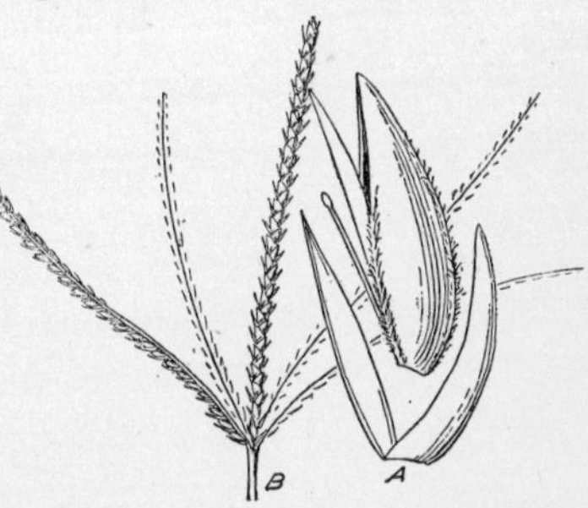

Fig. 48. A, spikelet of *Capriola Dactylon*, floret raised above the glumes; B, inflorescence.

mains in the prolonged rachilla, often with a rudimentary floret at its apex. The arrangement of the inflorescence (Fig. 48, B; three of the spikes indicated in skeleton only) is the same as in Eleusine.

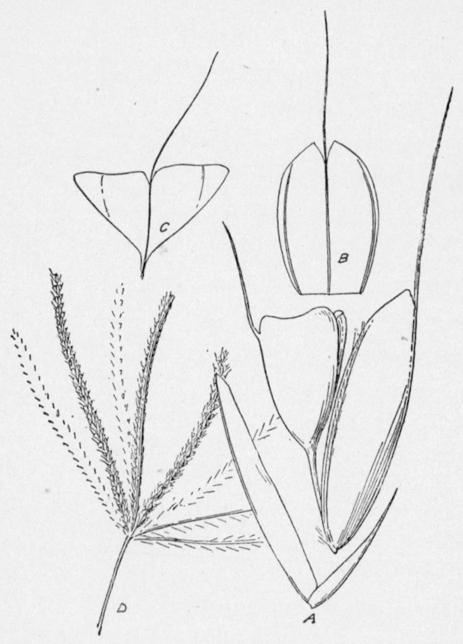

FIG. 49. A, spikelet of *Chloris latisquamea;* B, fertile lemma spread out; C, sterile lemma spread out; D, inflorescence.

Compare Figs. 48 and 49 (*Chloris latisquamea*). In the latter, the upper florets instead of being suppressed are developed into one or a few sterile florets, consisting of modified lemmas without paleas. Turn to Lesson III in which sterile florets are discussed (page 23). In Melica (Fig. 19) we had an example of such sterile florets, and in Chloris we have another. In each case, the sterile lemmas if spread out show their derivation from the ordinary fertile lemmas.

In grama grass, Bouteloua (Figs. 50 and 51), is found the greatest specialization of the sterile floret. It is often more prominent than the fertile floret and so modified that its derivation is not always obvious. The pattern of its lemma, however, is like that of the fertile one, 3-nerved, the nerves extending into awns (Figs. 50, C and 51, C.) The internerves are commonly broadened and reduced (as in Fig. 51, C), or even suppressed. There is usually a single such floret, but in some species there are two, or even three. A second sterile lemma when present may have a single awn or be awnless, or even nerveless (Fig. 51, D). In a few species the sterile floret sometimes incloses a palea and stamens. Note that in Bouteloua the spikes are not digitate, as in the foregoing genera, but are

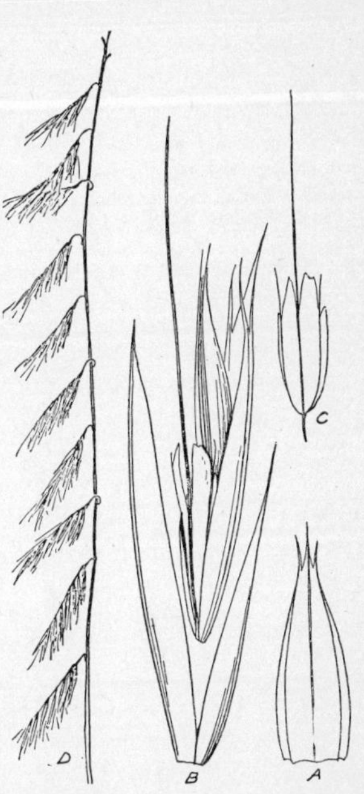

FIG. 50. A, spikelet of *Bouteloua curtipendula;* B, fertile lemma spread out; C, sterile lemma spread out; D, inflorescence.

racemose (Figs. 50, D, and 51, E); that is, the axis between the spikes is elongate instead of greatly reduced. (In Fig. 10, B, is shown a raceme of spikelets; in Bouteloua we have a raceme of spikes, each

Fig. 51. A, spikelet of *Bouteloua gracilis;* B, fertile lemma spread out; C, first sterile lemma spread out; D, second sterile lemma spread out; E, inflorescence.

composed of few to many sessile spikelets.) In *Bouteloua gracilis* (Fig. 51) and related species the florets, as is usual in this group, fall from the glumes, these remaining on the rachis. In *B. curtipendula* (Fig. 50) and its relatives, the entire spike falls from the main axis.

In an allied genus, Cathestecum (which looks like a diminutive Bouteloua) with but one species in the United States, the spikes consist of three spikelets crowded on the short rachis, the uppermost fertile, the two lower staminate or neuter. The spikes fall as a whole from the axis.

In Lesson III (page 24) it is stated that the position of sterile florets in the spikelets is the same in large series of related grasses. In the spikelets so far studied in this lesson the sterile florets are above the perfect one. There is a single exception to this rule in Campulosus, in which the two lower lemmas are well developed but empty, the third fertile, and the upper one to three empty, like the lower.

In two genera in this group, Spartina and Beckmannia, the spikelets fall entire. (See Lesson VI, page 44, on exceptions). In Spartina the spikelets are strictly 1-flowered; in Beckmannia they are usually 1-flowered, but sometimes a second floret is developed.

Throughout we have seen widely different forms, such as Eleusine and Bouteloua, connected by intermediate forms like Capriola and Chloris. Such an intermediate between pediceled spikelets, as in Bromus, Poa, and others of Lesson IV, and sessile spikelets, as in the group we are now studying, is found in Leptochloa, in which the spikelets are arranged along one side of the slender rachises, but are borne on very short pedicels. The spikelets of our other genera in this highly specialized group present no special difficulty, except those of buffalo-grass, to be studied later.

SUMMARY

In this group the spikelets are sessile in 1-sided spikes, solitary, digitate, or racemose. In most of the genera the upper florets are sterile, their lemmas greatly modified, or they are wholly suppressed.

REVIEW

Collect the inflorescence of Bermuda-grass, yard-grass, any of the grama-grasses, or of any available grass with 1-sided spikes. Note the arrangement of the spikes on the main axis; distinguish the individual spikelets and identify their parts.

LESSON IX

DIVERSELY SPECIALIZED SPIKELETS

In Lesson IV, Fig. 22 (page 31), we had an example of fertile and sterile spikelets in the same fascicle, the fascicle falling as a whole. Because the type of spikelet showed kinship with grasses having many-flowered laterally compressed spikelets, Achyrodes is placed with them, although in its fascicles falling as a whole it forms an exception. In the grasses we are about to study in the present lesson, clustered spikelets are the characteristic specialization.

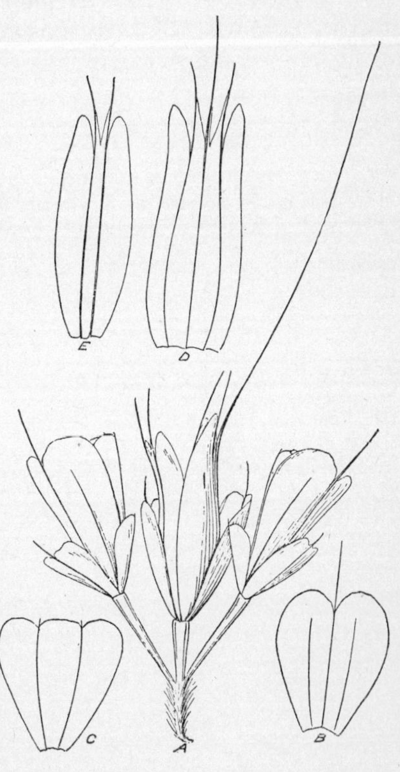

Fig. 52. A, fascicle of *Ægopogon tenellus;* B, lemma, and C, palea, spread out, of sterile spikelet; D, lemma and E, palea of perfect spikelet.

Examine Fig. 52 (Ægopogon) in which A represents a fascicle (spread apart) of one fertile and two sterile spikelets attached to the branch which falls with them. These little fascicles are racemose and nodding on the main axis.

In Hilaria (Fig. 53) the plan is the same, but the fascicles are sessile on the axis and erect, the spikelets are sessile in the fascicle, the glumes are elaborated

Fig. 53. A, fascicle of *Hilaria Belangeri;* B, glumes (inner face) of staminate spikelet; C, two views of perfect spikelet; D, fertile floret.

and very unsymmetrical, and the sterile spikelets have two florets. The species figured is the commonest one. The fascicles of some of the other species are even more fantastic than these. The glumes and lemma are always sharply folded and compressed laterally. In one species the glumes of the sterile spikelets are broad and fan-shaped, in another they are curiously lobed and awned. In all the species they are exceedingly variable, but in each they follow a general pattern. The glumes of the fertile floret are often slightly adnate to (grown to) those of the sterile spikelets, making the fascicle somewhat difficult to dissect. It is in such cases as this that the fundamental concept of the structure of a grass spikelet enables one to recognize the spikelet and its parts. So much elaboration for the production of a single grain is very exceptional in grasses, which as a whole tend to the elimination of non-essentials.

A third grass having spikelets in little fascicles is Nazia (see Fig. 54). This is probably not closely related to Ægopogon and Hilaria, but is commonly grouped with them because of its fascicles falling entire. This little bur-like fascicle is composed of two spikelets, both usually perfect (sometimes with a third reduced one). The minute first glumes are back to back, and the large second glumes, covered with stout hook-like hairs, face outward. Note that the glumes are not folded as in Ægopogon and Hilaria but convex. These spikelets afford an excellent example of spine-like hairs. Hairs are an outgrowth of the epidermis (skin) and have no connection with the fibrous structure of the plant. The "thorns" of the rose furnish a well-known

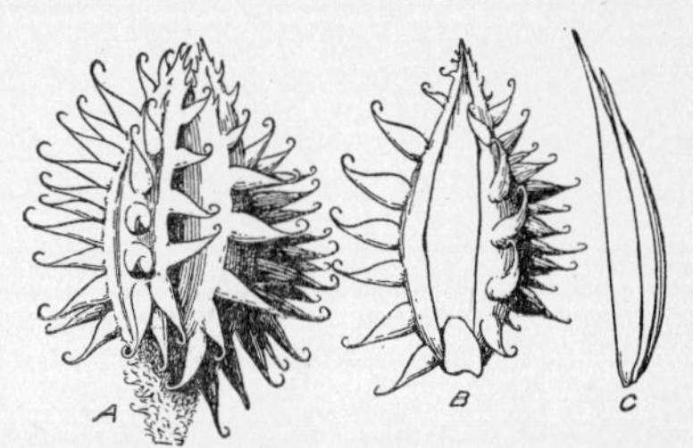

FIG. 54. A, bur-like fascicle of *Nazia aliena;* B, single spikelet; C, floret.

example. However stout they may be, they may readily be broken from the bark without tearing the wood. The thorns of hawthorns, plums, and locusts, on the contrary, however slender, can not be broken off. Being reduced branches, the woody fiber (vascular bundles) extends into them from the skeleton of the plant.

In all the spikelets figured heretofore the sterile florets when present were above the perfect floret. In a group of grasses represented by only three genera in the United States, the spikelets bear a pair of sterile florets below the single perfect floret and these fall attached to the fertile one. In sweet vernal-grass, or Anthoxanthum (Fig. 55) the sterile florets consist of empty lemmas unequally awned from the back and divided above the insertion of the awn. The fertile floret is much smaller, awnless, smooth, and shining. A beginner, in dissecting this spikelet, might mistake this fertile floret for the grain and so take the sterile florets for a lemma and a very peculiar palea. Whenever a spikelet or any of its parts seems to present a marked departure

Fig. 55. A, spikelet of *Anthoxanthum odoratum;* B, pair of sterile florets below the perfect floret; C, perfect floret.

from the normal type (such as a 1-awned palea would be), it is advisable to reëxamine and to reconsider. A close examination of this fertile floret will reveal the thin edges of the lemma infolding the palea. A grain may always be recognized by the embryo at the base on the back. (See Fig. 5, A).

In Torresia (called holy-grass, vanilla-grass, or Seneca-grass) the sterile florets are awnless and contain paleas and stamens. Like Anthoxanthum, the whole plant is fragrant. These are the grasses of which sweet-grass baskets are made.

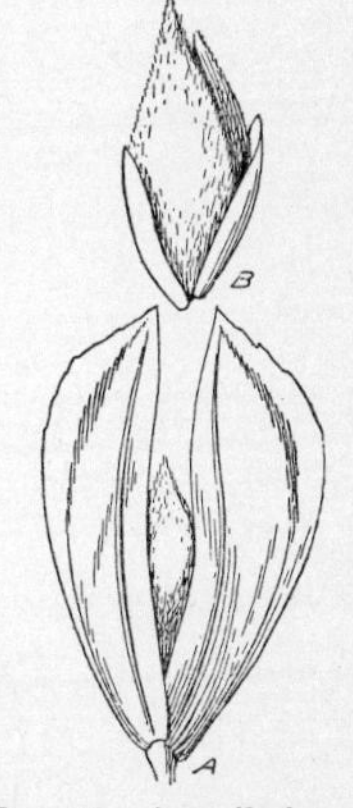

FIG. 56. A, spikelet of *Phalaris canariensis;* B, fertile floret with pair of small sterile florets attached at base.

In Phalaris the glumes are enlarged and strongly keeled or, as in canary-grass, *P. canariensis* (Fig. 56), wing-keeled, and the sterile florets are reduced to small empty lemmas. In one species, *P. minor*, the first sterile floret is reduced to a minute rudiment, and in the common reed canary-grass, *P. arundinacea*, both sterile lemmas are narrow and hairy.

In Lesson VII, Fig. 42 (page 50), we had an example of greatly reduced glumes. In rice, *Oryza sativa* (Fig. 57), the glumes are minute, and the lemma and palea are indurate (hardened) and compressed laterally. Some varieties of rice have an awned lemma. In an allied genus, Homalocenchrus (Fig. 58), the glumes are wholly suppressed.

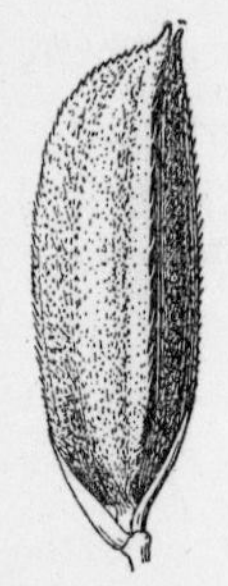

FIG. 57. Spikelet of rice (*Oryza sativa*).

FIG. 58. Spikelet of *Homalocenchrus oryzoides*.

In Lesson IV, Figs. 23 (page 32) and 24 (page 32), we had unisexual spikelets, the staminate and pistillate on distinct plants. Wild rice, *Zizania palustris* (Fig. 59, A and B), is monœcious, staminate and pistillate spikelets borne in the same panicle, the awnless staminate ones pendulous on the spreading lower branches, the awned pistillate ones erect on the ascending upper branches. In the pistillate spikelet the suppressed glumes are represented by a very shallow ridge around the base of the spikelet. The staminate flower consists of six stamens instead of three, as in the grasses studied heretofore. The palea of this spikelet is

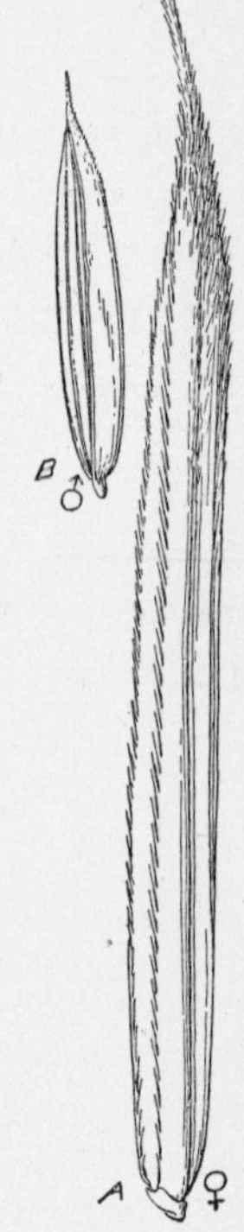

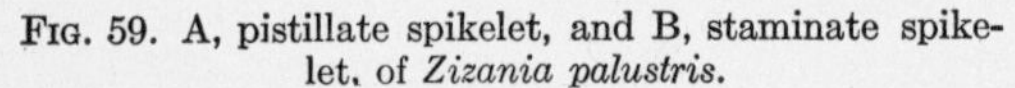

FIG. 59. A, pistillate spikelet, and B, staminate spikelet, of *Zizania palustris*.

anomalous in that it has three nerves. Throughout the grasses the palea has two nerves, rarely suppressed, as in Agrostis, where the palea itself is much reduced, or so close together as to be merged into one, but in no case are more than two nerves known. The problem presented by this spikelet has not been satisfactorily solved. It is possible that the two organs are, respectively, the second glume and the lemma, the first glume and the palea being suppressed. In the pistillate spikelet the palea is 2-nerved. In the perennial wild rice of the southeastern states, *Zizaniopsis miliacea*, this 3-nerved organ is present in both the staminate and pistillate spikelets, and in another related genus, Luziola, both bracts of the spikelets are several to many nerved.

SUMMARY

In the highly specialized spikelets studied in this lesson the various organs are identified (1) by their position, bearing in mind that the bracts of a spikelet are 2-ranked and alternate on the rachilla, and (2) by their resemblance to corresponding organs in allied grasses.

REVIEW

Hilaria, Nazia, and Ægopogon are found only in the Southwest, but the other grasses studied in this lesson are widespread. In any region in the United States will be found one or more of them. Collect any that are available, examine the inflorescence, distinguish the spikelets, and identify their parts.

If in a species of Phalaris but one sterile floret is found below the perfect one, how can you tell which of the pair is suppressed?

LESSON X

SPIKELETS WITH MEMBRANACEOUS GLUMES AND HARDENED FRUITS

All the spikelets heretofore studied have been more or less compressed laterally (that is, a detached spikelet under observation lies on its side, the two ranks of glumes and lemmas to right and left of the rachilla, as in Figs. 11–14) and, with relatively few exceptions, the articulation has been above the glumes, these remaining on the pedicel after the fall of the florets. These two characters in common pertain to more than half of all our grasses. In many of the laterally compressed spikelets the florets themselves are dorsally compressed (see Fig. 11, B). We come now to a lesser group, in which the spikelets are dorsally compressed (the spikelet under observation lying on its face or back, the two ranks above and below the rachilla). In this group of grasses the rachilla joints are usually so short that the glumes and lemmas are borne one immediately above the other. The rachilla is never prolonged beyond the base of the fertile floret, as in many of the spikelets heretofore studied.

Examine Fig. 60. Note that the first glume is much smaller than the second. Turn to Fig. 11 (page 25). In imagination, remove the glumes and all but the two lower florets. The result is comparable to the two florets (Fig. 60, C) of Panicum, but in this genus the lower floret is staminate or sterile, and its lemma and palea differ in form and texture from those of the perfect floret (Fig. 60, D). The sterile lemma (commonly termed the "third glume" in all but recent books) resembles the second glume and incloses a small thin palea, while the

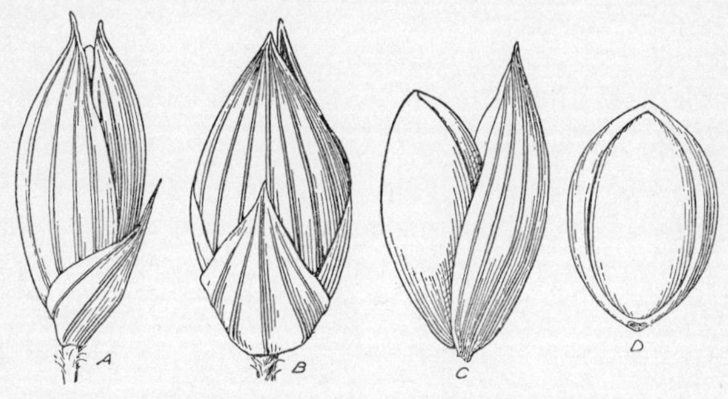

FIG. 60. A, spikelet of *Panicum miliaceum*, side view; B, same seen from the back; C, sterile and fertile florets removed from the glumes, side view; D, fertile floret.

fertile lemma is indurate, its nerves obscured in the thickened tissue, and firmly clasps a palea of like texture. At maturity the grain is inclosed in this fast-locked little case (the whole commonly termed the fruit) and germinates within it, sending its rootlet through a thin place near the base of the lemma (seen as a crescent-shaped depression at the back) and thrusting its sprout between the lemma and palea at the summit or side. In dissecting a spikelet of Panicum or its related genera the palea of the sterile floret often adheres to the palea side of the fruit (the mature fertile floret) as a small thin scale, difficult for the beginner to account for unless he understands the structure of the spikelet.

Fig. 61. A, two views of spikelet of *Syntherisma sanguinalis;* B, fertile floret; C, inflorescence.

This type of spikelet is characteristic of the large number of grasses forming the millet tribe. In Panicum the inflorescence is an open or contracted panicle. In crab-grass, *Syntherisma sanguinalis* (Fig. 61) and its relatives, the spikelets are borne in 1-sided racemes, much like those of Bermuda-grass (Fig. 48). In the crab-grasses the first glume is minute or suppressed, and the second is commonly much shorter than the sterile lemma and the fertile floret. The fertile lemma and its palea are less indurate than those of Panicum and the margin of the lemma is thin in texture and flat instead of being firm and inrolled, as in Panicum.

In Paspalum (Fig. 62) the spikelets are more like those of Panicum in texture, and the margin of the fertile lemma is firm and inrolled, as in that genus. The first glume is wholly suppressed except in a few species. The spikelets are subsessile in two rows on one side of a rachis, either single (Figs. 62 and 63, A)

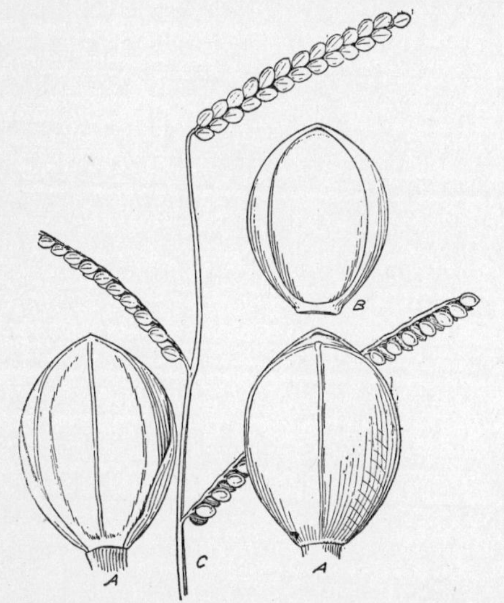

Fig. 62. A, two views of spikelet of *Paspalum læve;* B, fertile floret; C, inflorescence.

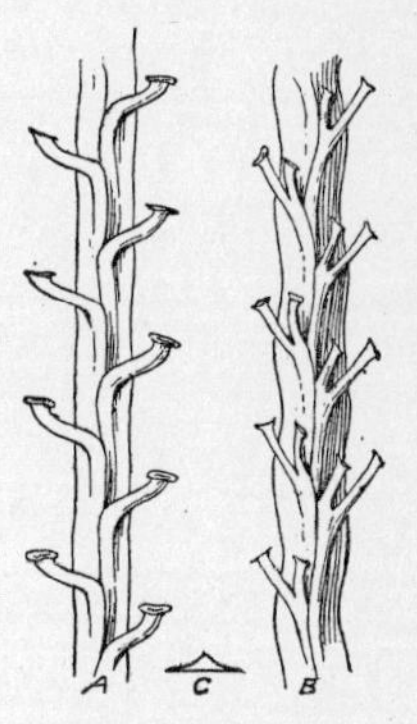

Fig. 63. A, rachis of *Paspalum læve*, spikelets removed; B, rachis of a Paspalum with paired spikelets; C, cross-section of rachis, showing raised center and thin margins.

or in pairs (Fig. 63, B). [In descriptions these are often referred to as 2-rowed or 4-rowed, respectively.] In species with paired spikelets some of the secondary ones (those next the center of the rachis) are always abortive. The racemes in Paspalum are sometimes solitary and sometimes digitate, as in Syntherisma, but more commonly they are racemose on the main axis (as in Fig. 62). The rachis is sometimes winged, and in a few species the broad wings fold up over the base of the spikelets.

In Reimarochloa (represented by but one species in the United States) the spikelets are arranged as in Paspalum, but both glumes are suppressed except in the uppermost spikelet. (Recall Lolium, Lesson V, Fig. 27, page 36). If it were not for its obvious relationship to Paspalum, in which an occasional first glume is developed in several species and regularly in a few, the spikelet of Reimarochloa might be taken to be strictly 1-flowered with only the first glume suppressed except in the terminal spikelet.

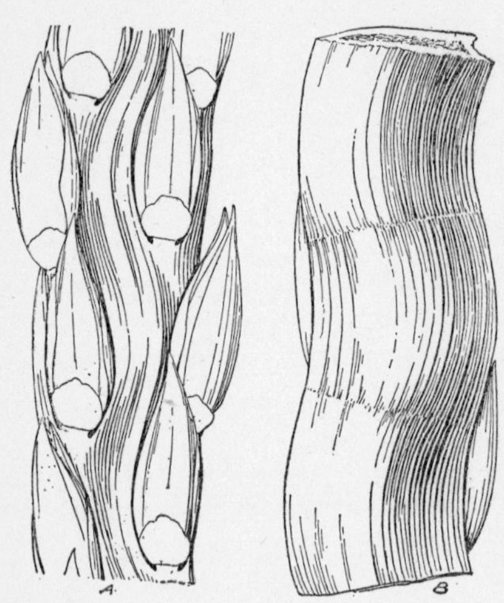

FIG. 64. A, part of raceme of *Stenotaphrum secundatum*, front view showing spikelets; B, back view of three joints.

In Paspalum we have seen a slightly broadened rachis (Fig. 63). In Stenotaphrum, or St. Augustine-grass (Fig. 64), the rachis is broad, thick, and corky, and the spikelets are partly embedded in it. At maturity the rachis breaks up into short joints with the spikelets attached. (Recall Lepturus, Lesson V, Fig. 28, page 37.)

In Syntherisma, Paspalum, Reimarochloa, and Stenotaphrum, with subsessile spikelets borne on one side of a rachis, the spikelets are placed with the back of the fertile lemma against the rachis, that is, with the first glume (developed or hypothetical), sterile lemma, and the palea of the fertile floret outward. In Axonopus (Fig. 65), Brachiaria, and Eriochloa the spikelets are reversed, the back of the fertile lemma being turned from the rachis and the palea toward it. In Axonopus the first glume is wholly suppressed. In Eriochloa (Fig. 66) the first glume is reduced to a minute sheath around the enlarged rachilla joint below the second glume and grown fast to it. The fertile lemma is tipped with a minute awn, which breaks off readily.

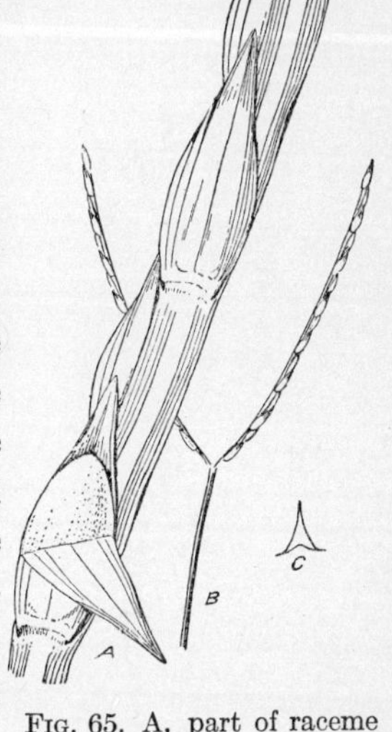

FIG. 65. A, part of raceme of *Axonopus furcatus;* B, inflorescence; C, cross-section of rachis.

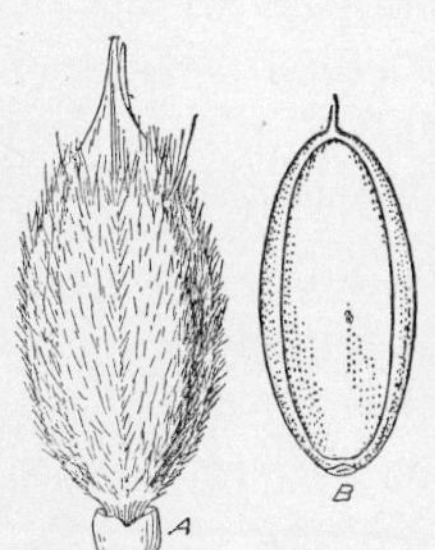

FIG. 66. A, spikelet of *Eriochloa punctata;* B, fertile floret.

In barnyard-grass, *Echinochloa Crusgalli*, is the same type of spikelet as in Panicum, but the second glume and sterile lemma are awned or awn-tipped, and the pointed tip of the palea is not inclosed in the lemma, which also is sharp-pointed. The glumes and sterile lemma bear spine-like hairs, but not so thick as those of Nazia.

Observe the diagrammatic panicle in Fig. 67, A. In imagination, remove all the terminal spikelets

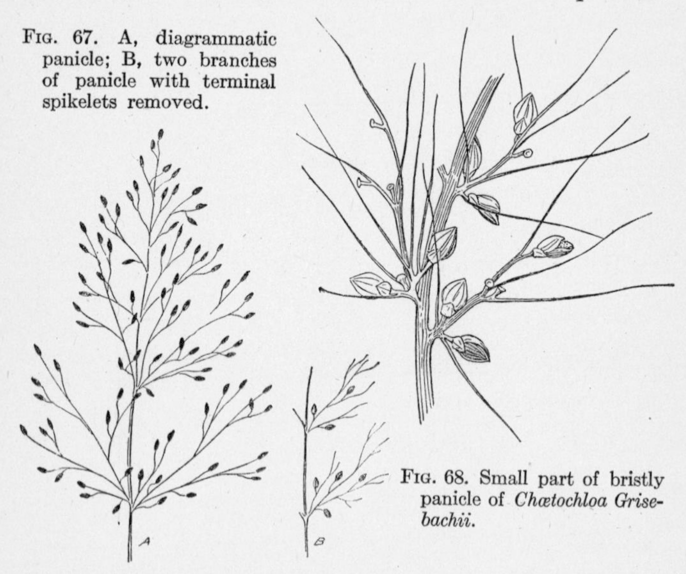

Fig. 67. A, diagrammatic panicle; B, two branches of panicle with terminal spikelets removed.

Fig. 68. Small part of bristly panicle of *Chætochloa Grisebachii.*

from a branch. The result is Fig. 67, B. Compare Fig. 68 with this. It will be seen that the bristles of the latter are branches of the panicle which are without spikelets at their tips but which bear subsessile spikelets at or toward their base. This modification of sterile branches and branchlets into rough bristles is found in the millets (Chætochloa), common millet, yellow foxtail, and green foxtail. These branchlets are the "involucre of bristles" referred to in many manuals and descriptions. The spikelets fall from their pedicels, as in Panicum, and the bristles remain on the axis. In most of the species the panicles are dense and spike-like, the spikelet-bearing branches fascicled and very short and the sterile ones, or bristles, long and slender. In yellow foxtail, *Chætochloa lutescens* (Fig. 69), the fascicle consists of several branches, only one of them spikelet-bearing, the others transformed into slender bristles.

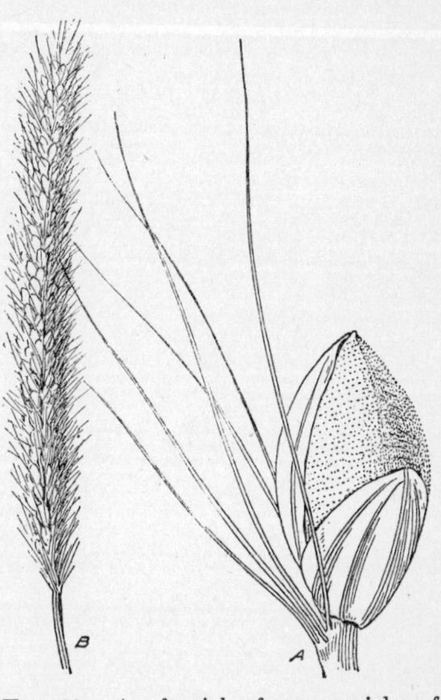

FIG. 69. A, fascicle from panicle of *Chætochloa lutescens;* B, spike-like panicle of same.

Between the ordinary panicle represented in Fig. 67 and the bristly spike-like one of yellow foxtail (Fig. 69, B) there is every degree of gradation.

A further specialization of sterile branches is shown in the sand-burs (Cenchrus). Compare Fig. 70 with Fig. 69, A. Instead of the nearly simple fascicle of branchlets found in the millets, the sand-burs have a complex fascicle of many compound branches. The primary branches disarticulate from the axis, and the whole fascicle, or bur, falls entire with the spikelet permanently inclosed, the grain eventually germinating within it. The simplest form of sand-bur is in *Cenchrus myosuroides* (Fig. 70). The structure of this will be comprehended if we conceive of

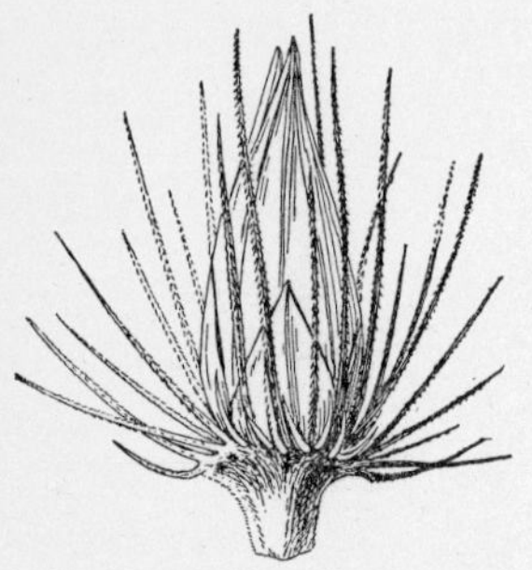

FIG. 70. Bur of *Cenchrus myosuroides.*

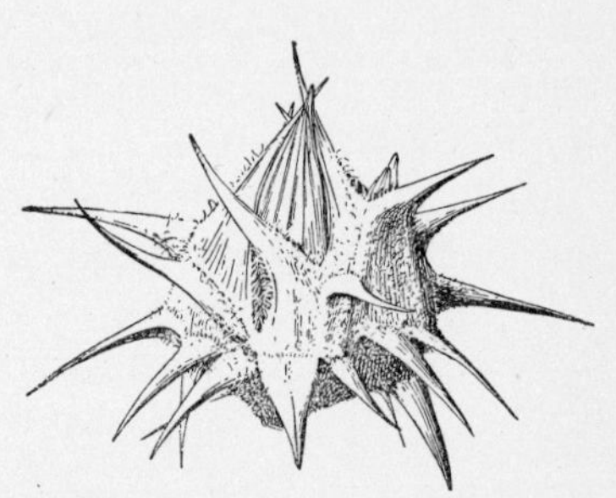

FIG. 71. Bur of *Cenchrus pauciflorus.*

a dense fascicle of branches with but one of them bearing a single sessile spikelet, the others branching at the base and surrounding the spikelet-bearing one. In the common inland sand-bur, *Cenchrus pauciflorus* (Fig. 71), the sterile branches are much thickened and flattened and are grown together below, their free summits sharp and spine-like. The numerous secondary branchlets, in the form of stout spines, spread from the body of the bur formed by the cohesion of the main branches surrounding the one or few sessile spikelets.

In all the seed-bearing spikelets so far examined, the stamens and stigmas project at flowering time, resulting in cross fertilization of the ovules. A few grasses bear cleistogamous (close-fertilized) as well as openly fertilized spikelets. Such spikelets do not open, and there is usually but a single small stamen which empties its pollen directly on the short stigmas. The grain is larger than that of open-fertilized spikelets. Two of our native grasses, forming the genus Amphicarpon, related to Panicum, are remarkable in that they produce large cleistogamous spikelets underground from subterranean branches (Fig. 72). The plants also bear terminal panicles of ordinary and much smaller spikelets, but these seldom perfect seed.

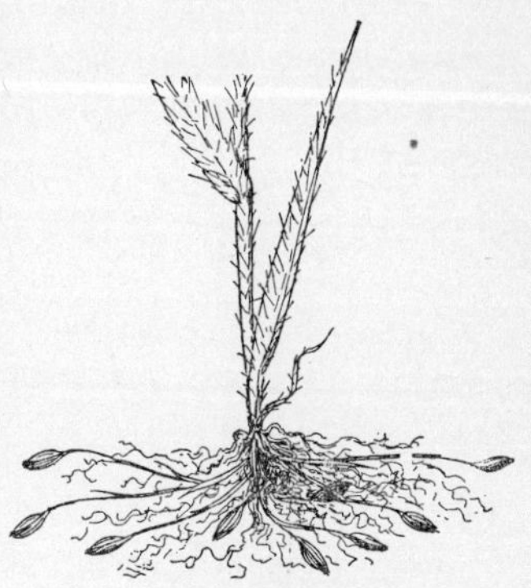

Fig. 72. Base of plant of *Amphicarpon Purshii.*

SUMMARY

In Paniceæ, the millet tribe, the spikelets fall entire. They bear one perfect floret with a sterile floret below it. The lemma and palea of the perfect floret are indurate. The sterile lemma resembles the second glume, the two simulating a pair of glumes, while the first glume is small and looks like an additional one (in some older works it is called the accessory valve or glume) or is entirely suppressed. The genera differ chiefly in the arrangement of the spikelets in the inflorescence. In a few genera some of the panicle branches are without spikelets and are transformed into bristles or burs.

REVIEW

Collect the inflorescence of broom-corn millet, old witch-grass, or of as many species of Panicum as are available, and dissect the spikelets. Collect heads of barnyard-grass and compare the spikelets with those of Panicum. Compare the spine-like hairs with those of Nazia, Fig. 54.

Collect the inflorescence of crab-grass and of any species of Paspalum available; note the arrangement of spikelets and compare the form and texture of the fruit (fertile floret) with that of Panicum.

Collect heads of common millet or of yellow or green foxtail. Remove enough branches from the axis to show clearly the form and arrangement of the few remaining.

If available, examine a sand-bur, splitting the bur with a sharp knife.

LESSON XI

PAIRED SPIKELETS WITH HARDENED GLUMES AND THIN LEMMAS

In the sorghum tribe, which we are about to study, the spikelet, as in the millet tribe, falls entire and is dorsally compressed, but the glumes are hardened and the lemmas thin, while in the millet tribe the glumes are thin and the fertile lemma and palea are hardened. The glumes entirely inclose the two florets. The midnerve of the first glume is commonly suppressed, while a pair of nerves near the margin is often prominent and sometimes keeled, or even winged. The second glume may be like the first or the midnerve may be slightly keeled. The lower floret consists of an empty lemma only, the upper of a perfect flower with a small thin often awned lemma (sometimes so small as to appear like a bit of membrane at the base of the awn) and a minute palea (sometimes suppressed).

Examine Fig. 73, A, and compare it with Figs. 21 (p. 30), 22 (p. 31), 30 (p. 40), 40 (p. 49), 52 (p. 61), and 53 (p. 62). In all the figures referred to, fertile spikelets are associated with sterile ones. These are grouped in various ways. In the sorghum tribe the typical arrangement is a jointed raceme with a sessile perfect spikelet and a pediceled sterile spikelet (staminate or neuter) at each joint, the rachis disarticulating at the summit of each joint, this and the pedicel of the sterile spikelet remaining attached at their base to the perfect spikelet as a pair of little stalks. In this group of grasses specialization consists chiefly in modifications of the axes of inflorescence and secondarily in the modification of the spikelets. In Fig. 73, A (Johnson-grass, *Holcus halepensis*), are two views of a single joint, consisting of the sessile perfect spikelet with the attached rachis joint and the pedicel with its staminate spikelet. Fig. 73, B, is a diagram of a raceme of four such joints and 73, C, a diagram of the rachis and pedicels, the spikelets removed and the points of disarticulation shown by dotted lines. In sorghum, or Holcus, these little racemes are borne on the ultimate branchlets of a panicle (Fig. 73, D).

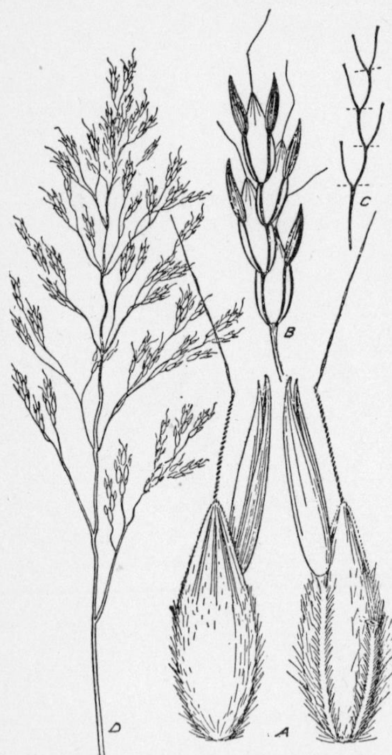

FIG. 73, A, two views of single joint of raceme of *Holcus halepensis;* B, diagram of raceme of four joints; C, diagram of rachis and pedicels; D, inflorescence.

In the closely related Indian-grass, Sorghastrum, the racemes are reduced to one or two joints, and the sterile spikelets are wholly suppressed, the slender hairy pedicel alone being developed.

Compare Fig. 74, A, a diagrammatic single joint of *Erianthus saccharoides*, with Fig. 73, A, and Fig. 74, B, three joints of a long raceme, with Fig. 73, B. It will be seen that, while the spikelets are paired, the pediceled spikelet is as large as the sessile one and, like it, is awned. In this genus the pediceled spikelet is usually perfect. The racemes are long and slender and copiously hairy, and are crowded on a stout main axis forming large, dense, woolly panicles. In sugar-cane the inflorescence is like that of Erianthus, but the spikelets are awnless.

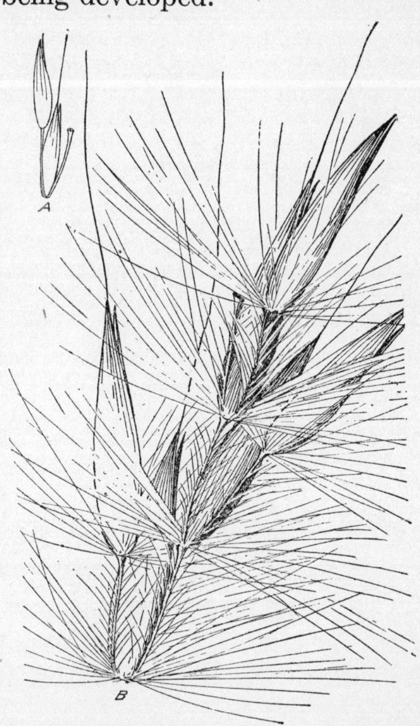

Fig. 74, A, diagram of single joint of raceme of *Erianthus saccharoides;* B, three joints of raceme.

Examine Fig. 75, A, a joint of a raceme of one of the broom sedges (*Andropogon scoparius*). It will be seen to have the same general plan as a joint of sorghum, and the racemes, shown in Fig. 75, B, though slender and flexuous, are in structure similar to the racemes of sorghum. The entire inflorescence, however, is very different. In sorghum and Erianthus the inflorescence is a leafless terminal panicle, such as is common in grasses. The diagrammatic inflorescence (Fig. 75, B) shows that the racemes of the broom-sedge are borne on numerous slender leafy branches arising in the axils of leaves on the main culm or branches, the whole forming a compound inflorescence. The leaves, especially the ultimate ones immediately below the racemes, are mostly reduced to bladeless sheaths and are sometimes bright colored. Such transformed leaves subtending or surrounding single inflorescences are commonly termed spathes.

FIG. 75. A, single joint of raceme of *Andropogon scoparius*; B, small part of compound inflorescence.

In some species the racemes are partly inclosed

in the spathes. The racemes may be solitary (that is, one to a branch, as shown) or two to several, digitate, on a single branch. In some species the sterile spikelet is suppressed, only the pedicel being developed. In a few species of Andropogon the racemes are in leafless panicles, as in Erianthus, but the pediceled spikelets are sterile and awnless.

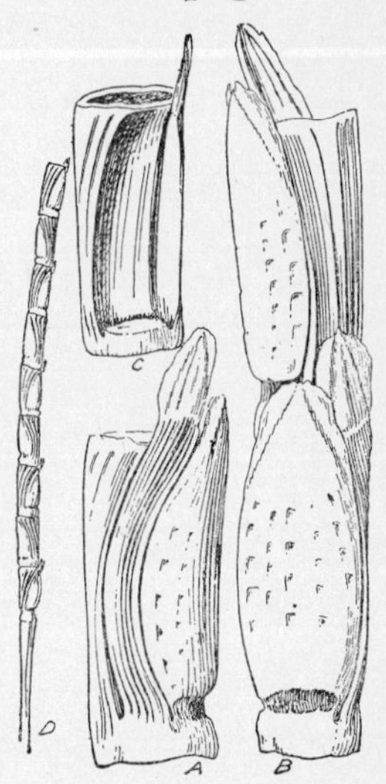

FIG. 76, A, single joint of raceme of *Manisuris cylindrica;* B, another view of two joints; C, inner face of rachis joint and pedicel, spikelet removed; D, part of cylindrical many-jointed raceme.

Examine Fig. 76, A (*Manisuris cylindrica*), and compare it with 73, A. In Holcus and Erianthus the rachis joint and the pedicel of the second spikelet are about equal in thickness. In Fig. 75 the rachis joint is stouter than the pedicel. In Manisuris the rachis joint is greatly thickened and hollowed out below on the inner face. (See Fig. 28, p. 37, for an earlier example of a thickened rachis.) The pedicel of the sterile spikelet is also thickened, but much less so, and the two lie close together (instead of spread apart, as in Figs. 73 to 75) and entirely cover the second-glume side of the spikelet which fits into the cavity formed by the rachis joint and pedicel. Fig. 76, C, shows the inner faces of the rachis joint and pedicel, the perfect spikelet removed. The spikelets are awnless and the marginal nerves of the first glume are winged at the summit. This inflorescence and that of Lepturus (Fig. 28) are so similar in appearance and function, disjointing with the mature seed permanently attached, that the student may wonder why they are placed in tribes so remote as the barley grasses and sorghum. The two illustrate what is not seldom shown in nature, that very different structures may arrive at the same function, although the forms from which they are derived were very remote. The inflorescence of Lepturus is a spike, and its spikelet shows it to be a reduced and specialized relative of Lolium. The inflorescence of Manisuris is a raceme with two spikelets at a joint, one pediceled, and the perfect spikelet not greatly different from that of sorghum.

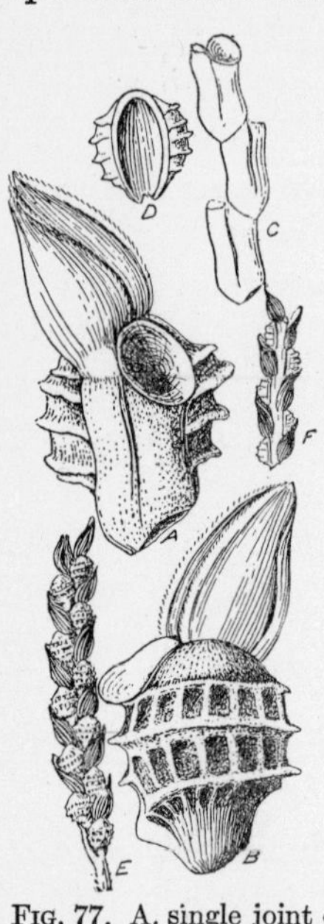

Fig. 77. A, single joint of raceme of *Rytilix granularis;* B, reverse view; C, diagram of rachis and pedicels of three joints of raceme, spikelets removed; D, view of inner face of first glume of sessile spikelet; E, raceme; F, reverse view.

We have just observed the rachis joint and pedicel lying closely pressed together. In Rytilix (Fig. 77, A) they are adnate (grown together). Examine the diagram of three joints with the spikelets removed (Fig. 77, C) and note that the rachis joints (the thicker parts) form a central axis with the pedicels borne on alternate sides, just as they are in Holcus (Fig. 73, C). In this raceme we have just the reverse of the arrangement of Manisuris. In that, the fertile spikelet fits into a cavity formed by the rachis joint and pedicel while in Rytilix the rachis joint and pedicel fit into a cavity formed by the fertile spikelet. (See Fig. 77, D, showing the inside face of the first glume of the perfect spikelet, and examine the two views of the joints, A and B, and the two views of the raceme, E and F). The sterile spikelet is well developed but usually contains no flower. The perfect spikelet with its peculiar gray, ridged and pitted, subglobose first glume suggests the achene of some species of Scleria (a sedge). The whole inflorescence is very unlike that of any other known grass.

Return to Fig. 73, A, and compare with it Fig. 78, A (*Rhaphis pauciflora*), which shows a raceme reduced to a single joint consisting of the sessile perfect spikelet and two pediceled sterile spikelets, the rachis joint (found in Holcus and the others studied) often being replaced by a second pedicel and sterile spikelet. This second sterile spikelet is not always developed. In Rhaphis this 1-jointed raceme has a sharp hairy callus at the base. Fig. 78, B (the base of a raceme and the summit of a branch, the hairs removed), shows the source of this callus. The racemes are borne on the long slender branches of a spreading panicle (Fig. 78, D) which disarticulate obliquely below the raceme, the line of articulation bordered by a dense brush of hairs (Fig. 78, C). The

Fig. 78. A, one-jointed raceme of *Rhaphis pauciflora;* B, base of raceme and summit of branch; C, hairy summit of branch from which raceme has fallen; D, inflorescence.

Fig. 79. A, single joint of raceme of *Heteropogon contortus;* B, perfect spikelet from which sterile spikelet has fallen; C, base of fertile spikelet and its callus; D, raceme; E, diagram of raceme; F, diagram of rachis and pedicels of four joints of raceme.

sterile spikelets with their pedicels fall off before the maturity of the perfect spikelet, which, with its hairy callus and long awn, closely resembles a mature floret of Stipa (Fig. 45).

In Heteropogon (Fig. 79) is a more complicated arrangement. In A is shown a joint of the raceme, consisting of the sessile perfect awned spikelet and the pediceled large pale sterile spikelet, with the short hairy rachis joint below forming a pointed callus. In Fig. 79, C, is seen the base of the fertile spikelet and the callus, with enough hairs removed to expose the very base of the pedicel, which has fallen with the sterile spikelet, and (to the left) the oblique scar from which the rachis joint next above has disarticulated. The articulation is at the base of the rachis joint instead of at the summit, as in Holcus and the others (Figs. 73–77), and forms a callus to the spikelet next above. The rachis joints are very short and the fertile spikelets (except their awns) are hidden by the overlapping sterile spikelets, the long flexuous awns forming a tangle beyond the end of the raceme (Fig. 79, D). Besides having this modified rachis and large unsymmetrical sterile spikelets, the raceme of Heteropogon presents a further modification in that its lower two or three pairs of spikelets are all sterile, instead of each pair consisting of a perfect and a sterile one, as typical for the sorghum tribe. In these lower pairs the sessile spikelet is staminate and the pediceled one empty, but both have large unsymmetrical glumes and appear to be alike. Examine the diagram of the raceme (Fig. 79, E, the rachis greatly lengthened to show the structure and arrows indicating the points of disarticulation) and contrast it with Fig. 73, B. Fig.

79, F, is a diagram of the rachis of four joints, showing the points of disarticulation. Contrast it with Fig. 73, C.

The mature fertile spikelets of Rhaphis and Heteropogon closely resemble mature fruits of Stipa and function in the same way, disseminating the seed by attaching themselves by their sharp calluses to passing animals and securing their hold by the untwisting and twisting of their hygroscopic (moisture-sensitive) awns. They afford another example of the same function performed by different organs.

SUMMARY

The grasses of the sorghum tribe have spikelets with hardened glumes and thin lemmas. Typically they are arranged in pairs, one sessile and perfect, the other pediceled and sterile on a jointed rachis, forming racemes. In several genera the rachis is elaborately modified.

REVIEW

Collect the inflorescence of Johnson-grass and of any of the broom-sedges. Break the raceme into single joints, noting the points at which it readily separates. Examine the spikelets and the rachis and distinguish the rachis joint from the pedicel.

If you had a panicle of Rhaphis (Fig. 78, D) from which all the sterile spikelets with their pedicels had fallen, how would you know it was not a species of Stipa?

Make diagrams of the inflorescence of any available species of the sorghum tribe.

LESSON XII

HIGHLY SPECIALIZED UNISEXUAL SPIKELETS

EXAMINE Fig. 80, gama-grass (*Tripsacum dactyloides*). This grass is monœcious (see p. 23). The pistillate spikelets are borne on the lower part of the one to three stout digitate racemes and the staminate spikelets on the upper part of the same racemes (Fig. 80, D). The part of the rachis bearing the staminate spikelets is relatively slender and falls off after flowering time; the part bearing the pistillate spikelets is greatly thickened and disarticulates with the spikelets permanently embedded in the joints. Fig. 80, A, shows two joints with spikelets embedded; B, a

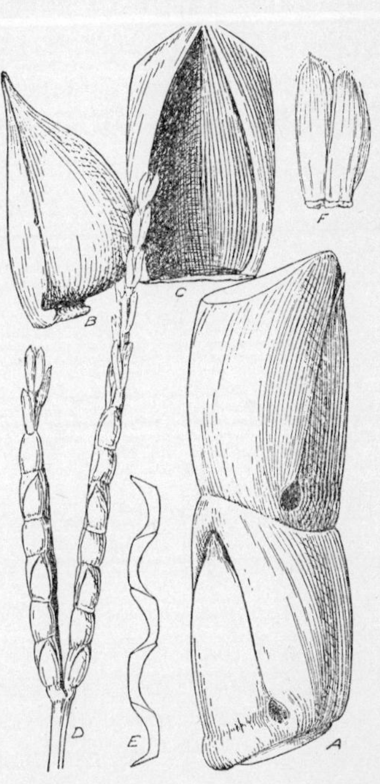

FIG. 80. A, two joints of pistillate part of raceme of *Tripsacum dactyloides;* B, spikelet removed from the joint; C, rachis joint from which spikelet has been removed; D, inflorescence; E, diagram of rachis of pistillate part; F, pair of staminate spikelets.

spikelet removed from its joint; C, the joint from which a spikelet has been removed; and E, a diagram of the rachis. Compare the joints with those of Manisuris (Fig. 76). Note that in Tripsacum the pistillate part is a simple spike with no vestige of a second spikelet. The structure of the spikelet is similar to that of spikelets of the sorghum tribe, having firm glumes (the first hard and like the rachis joint in texture), a thin sterile lemma, and a very thin fertile lemma and palea. The staminate spikelets are in pairs (Fig. 80, F) and one of each pair is usually on a very short pedicel. The glumes are much like those of different species of Andropogon; both florets are staminate, their lemmas and paleas thin.

Indian corn, or maize (*Zea Mays*), the most highly specialized grass known, is believed to be related to Tripsacum. It is monœcious, but the staminate and pistillate spikelets are borne in distinct inflorescences. The staminate spikelets are in pairs on a slender rachis forming racemes, these arranged in a panicle, the "tassel," at the summit of the culm. The pistillate spikelets are in pairs, crowded in 8 to 16 rows (rarely more) always an even number, on a greatly thickened compound axis, the "cob," borne in the axils of the leaves and enveloped in numerous leafy bracts ("husks"), the long styles (the "silk") protruding from the summit, the whole called the "ear." The staminate spikelets (Fig. 81, C) are much like those of Tripsacum and contain two staminate florets. The pistillate spikelets stand at right angles to their axis, the cob (Fig. 81, A). The glumes are minute, scarcely covering the ovary at flowering time (Fig. 81, B), and in the ripened grain remain as chaff on the cob, the greatly enlarged grain being naked. This grain, "a kernel of corn," remains on the axis until loosened by force.

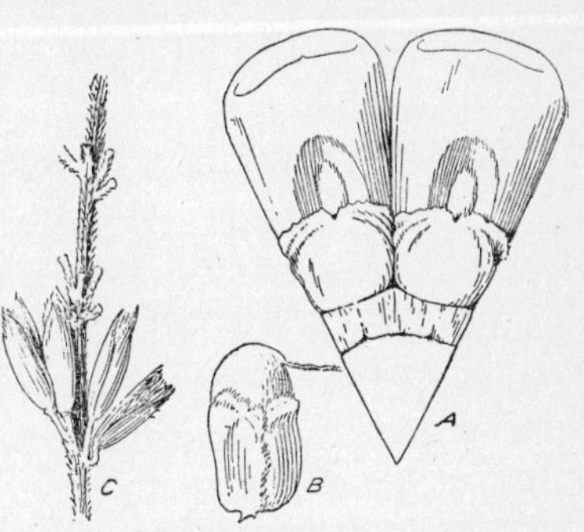

Fig. 81, A, part of cross-section of an ear of corn, *Zea Mays*, showing two pistillate spikelets standing at right angles to their axis (the cob); B, pistillate spikelet about flowering time; C, part of raceme of staminate spikelets.

Indian corn is known only in cultivation. The problem of its origin has not yet been solved. We only know that it originated somewhere in America, probably on the uplands of the tropics. It was widely cultivated by the aborigines when the western continents were discovered. The problem of the morphology of the ear of corn has not yet been satisfactorily solved, but it is not at all difficult to recognize the individual spikelets, both staminate and pistillate.

The student who has come this far will find it possible to dissect the inflorescence of any of our grasses, with the possible exception of buffalo-grass, and to distinguish the spikelets and the different organs.

Buffalo-grass (*Bulbilis dactyloides*) is placed in the same tribe as the grama-grasses (page 57), but it has been left until the last, so that the student might have greater experience to draw on. It is diœcious (p. 23), and the staminate and pistillate inflorescences are strikingly different. (Recall Fig. 24, p. 32).

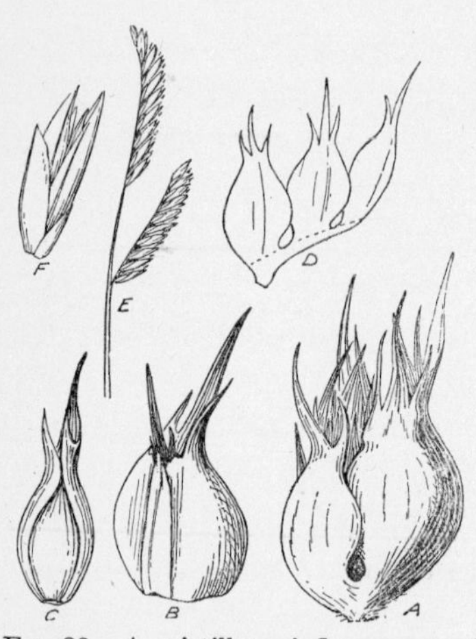

Fig. 82. A, pistillate inflorescence of *Bulbilis dactyloides;* B, pistillate spikelet cut from the rachis; C, pistillate floret; D, diagram of half a head, showing one of the two rows of spikelets; E, staminate inflorescence; F, staminate spikelet.

Examine Fig. 82, B, showing a pistillate spikelet with a small narrow first glume and a very large, broad, 3-toothed second glume entirely infolding the body of the floret. The floret, removed from the glume, is shown in Fig. 82, C. Its 3-toothed lemma approaches in form the lemma of some of the grama-grasses. (Compare with Fig. 50, B). This pistillate spikelet as presented is not at all puzzling, the large thick second glume with overlapping edges entirely inclosing the floret being the only remarkable feature. These spikelets, however, are borne in the curious inflorescence shown in Fig. 82, A. These little hard white heads are borne, mostly two together, on a very short slender axis, in the axils of broadened sheaths at the summit of short culms and very much overtopped by the blades. If we cut off the base of one of these little heads we have three to five such spikelets, as shown in Fig. 82, B, which had been held rigidly together by the hard thickened base, the overlapping backs of the second glumes forming a thick white wall surmounted by their green-toothed summits. The base can be nothing but a rachis, shortened, broadened, and thickened, though all trace is lost of the junction of the spikelets and the rachis. Fig. 82, D, is a diagram of half a head, showing one of the two rows of spikelets. Compare this with Fig. 51, E, showing a great number of spikelets on an elongate rachis. As in *Bouteloua gracilis* the spikelets stand nearly at right angles to the rachis and the first glume is inward, that is, it would be against the rachis, as in Bermuda-grass, if the spikelets were appressed. The difficulty the student encounters in comprehending the pistillate inflorescence of buffalo-grass is not so much due to its complexity as to the difficulty of dissecting the rigid little structure, and also to the suppression or deformity of some of the organs. When spikelets are closely crowded, as in the Cenchrus bur, in some species of millet, and in buffalo-grass, some of them are nearly always deformed from pressure. In buffalo-grass one or two of the spikelets in a head are not fully developed. The first glume is commonly reduced to a minute scale in two or three of the spikelets, and sometimes it is suppressed.

The staminate inflorescence (Fig. 82, E) resembles the spikes of grama-grass (Fig. 51, E) but the spikelets (Fig. 82, F) are awnless, and the second floret is well developed and contains a staminate flower.

SUMMARY

In the case of greatly modified structures the different organs are to be interpreted by their relative position and by their analogy to corresponding organs in related grasses.

REVIEW

Collect the inflorescence of Tripsacum if available, disjoint it and dissect the spikelets.

Examine a very young ear of corn and note that the spikelets are always in pairs (consequently an ear of corn always has an even number of rows). Distinguish the glumes and lemmas. Examine the staminate spikelets.

If available, collect buffalo-grass and dissect the staminate and pistillate inflorescence, preparing the latter by boiling it a few moments in water to which a few drops of glycerine have been added. When no glume but the large thickened one is found in the pistillate spikelet of buffalo-grass, how do you know which glume that is?

DIAGRAMMATIC SUMMARY OF THE PRIMARY CHARACTERS OF THE TRIBES

SERIES I.—POATÆ

Spikelets laterally compressed; florets mostly falling from the persistent glumes

1. FESTUCEÆ, fescue tribe

Spikelets many-flowered.
Glumes relatively small.
Lemmas awned from summit or awnless.
Inflorescence a panicle.
[Contains fescues, brome-grasses, and blue-grass.]

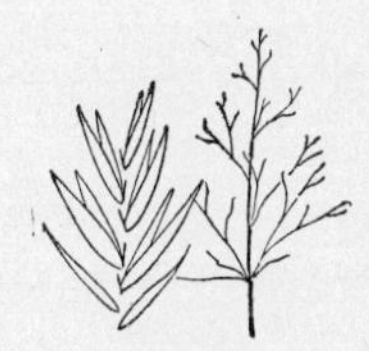

FIG. 83.

2. HORDEÆ, barley tribe

Spikelets 1- to many-flowered, sessile on opposite sides of a jointed rachis, forming a spike.
Rachis rather than spikelets specialized.
Inflorescence a solitary spike.
[Contains wheat, rye, and barley.]

FIG. 84.

3. AVENEÆ, oat tribe

Like Festuceæ, but glumes enlarged and florets fewer in number.
Rachilla joints short.
Lemmas awned from the back.
Inflorescence a panicle.
[Contains oats.]

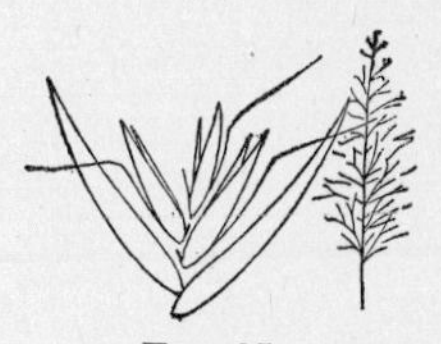

FIG. 85.

4. Agrostideæ, timothy tribe

Like Festuceæ reduced to its lowest terms; spikelets 1-flowered.
Lemmas awnless or awned, the awn from back or summit.
Glumes sometimes awned, sometimes suppressed.
Inflorescence a panicle.
[Contains redtop and timothy.]

Fig. 86.

5. Chlorideæ, grama tribe

Spikelets 1- to several-flowered, sessile on one side of a continuous rachis.
All but the lowest floret commonly sterile and variously modified.
Inflorescence of two to several 1-sided spikes, solitary, racemose or digitate.
[Contains grama-grasses.]

Fig. 87.

6. Nazieæ, curly-mesquite tribe.

Spikelets 1- or 2-flowered, in fascicles, the whole falling from the main axis entire.
[Not a natural tribe, some of the genera included not being closely related.]

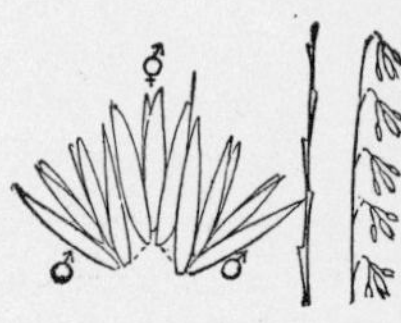

Fig. 88.

7. PHALARIDEÆ, canary-grass tribe

Spikelets with one perfect floret and two sterile florets below, these falling attached to the fertile floret.
Inflorescence a panicle.
[Contains canary-grass and sweet vernal-grass.]

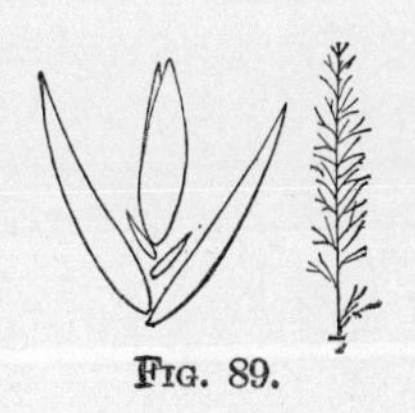

FIG. 89.

8. ORYZEÆ, rice tribe

Spikelets 1-flowered, falling from the pedicel entire.
Glumes reduced or suppressed.
Inflorescence a panicle.
[Contains rice.]

FIG. 90.

9. ZIZANIEÆ, Indian rice tribe

Plants monœcious.
Spikelets 1-flowered, falling entire.
Glumes suppressed.
Inflorescence a panicle.
[Wild or Indian rice.]

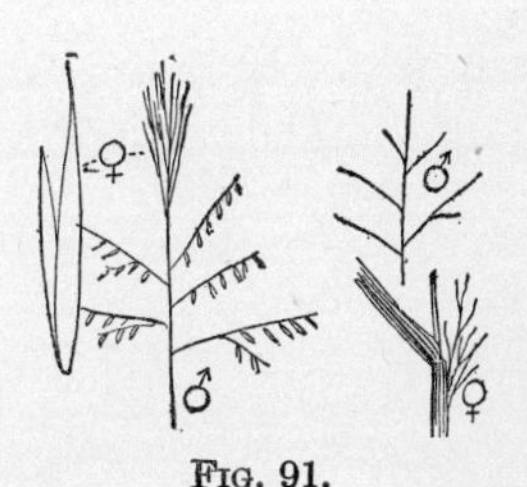

FIG. 91.

SERIES II.—PANICATÆ

Spikelets dorsally compressed, falling entire, singly or together with parts of the axis.

10. Paniceæ, millet tribe

Spikelets with one perfect terminal floret and a sterile floret below.

Rachilla joints very short.

Glumes membranaceous, the first small, suppressed in some genera; sterile lemma like the second glume, the two appearing like a pair of glumes.

Fertile lemma and palea indurate.

Inflorescence a panicle or of one to many racemes, these digitate or racemose on the main axis.

[Contains millets and crab-grasses.]

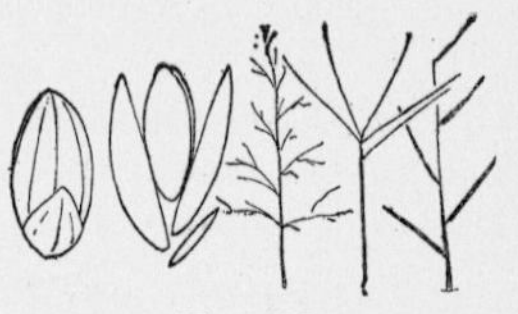

Fig. 92.

11. ANDROPOGONEÆ, sorghum tribe

Spikelets paired, one perfect and sessile, the other sterile and pedicellate, borne on a jointed rachis.

Fertile spikelets with one perfect terminal floret and a sterile lemma below; falling with joints of rachis and sterile pediceled spikelet attached.

Glumes indurate, inclosing the florets; lemmas very thin; palea often suppressed.

[Contains sugar-cane, Johnson-grass and broom-sedges.]

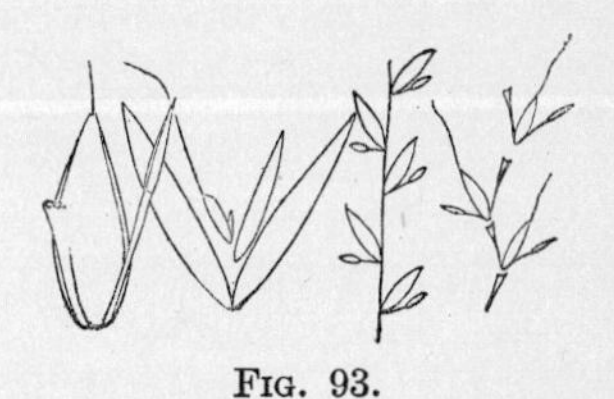

FIG. 93.

12. TRIPSACEÆ, corn tribe

Plants monœcious.

Pistillate spikelets with one perfect terminal floret and a sterile lemma below, falling embedded in the joints of the rachis. Persistent on the thick compound axis in Zea.)

Staminate spikelets 2-flowered in pairs, racemose.

[Contains gama-grass and Indian corn.]

FIG. 94.

GENERAL INFORMATION FOR THE BEGINNER

It is hoped that after completing the twelve lessons the student will be eager to study and identify the grasses of his region.

To aid the beginner in the study of the plant, the following outline is offered, suggesting points to be observed:

Outline for Study of a Grass Plant

Duration—Annual: Winter annual, summer annual.

Perennial: Without rhizomes (with or without winter rosette); with rhizomes (these short or long, thick, knotty, or slender).

Habit—Erect, ascending, prostrate, geniculate, creeping, rooting at nodes, or stoloniferous. Tufted or culms few or solitary.

Culm—Height; slender or robust; simple or branching (from upper nodes, lower nodes, all nodes); glabrous, scabrous, or pubescent (throughout or below nodes or inflorescence).

Nodes: Glabrous or pubescent (hairs appressed, spreading, retrorse, i. e., pointing backward).

Sheaths: Close, loose, or spreading; glabrous or pubescent (note margin and summit); open (as common) or closed.

Ligule: Length; membranaceous; hairy (stiff or delicate); obsolete.

Blades: Erect or spreading, length and width. Shape: Rounded, clasping or narrowed at base; flat, folded, or involute. Texture: Thin, thick, rigid, lax. Surface: Glabrous, pubescent (pilose, villous, hispid), scabrous (note each surface and margin).

Inflorescence—Terminal only on main culm and branches, or axillary also. Simple or compound. Panicle, size (length and width), loose or compact, few-flowered or many-flowered, nodding or erect. Raceme, size, etc. Spike, size, etc.

Axis of panicle: Size, pubescence, etc.; branches solitary, fascicled or whorled, flexuous or stiff, ascending, spreading or reflexed.

Axis of raceme or spike: Continuous or disjointing; slender, stout, narrow, winged; pubescence.

Spikelet—Pediceled or sessile; laterally or dorsally compressed; falling entire, alone, or with joints of axis; florets falling from the glumes; number of florets.

Glumes: Similar or unlike; size (compared to spikelet, one-half, one-third, etc.); shape, awned, toothed, etc.; texture, nerving, pubescence.

Lemma: Fertile or sterile, size, shape, texture, pubescence.

Palea: Flower bearing or empty, size (sometimes obsolete), shape, texture.

It will further the student's self-training if he writes down the characters of the first few grasses studied and of any particularly puzzling or interesting later ones, making drawings of the spikelet and its parts or diagrams of complicated inflorescences. One should not hesitate to make drawings merely because he "can not draw." However crude a sketch may be it is of great value, not only as a record of observations, but for its training in powers of observation. The one who "never could draw" is the very one who should make frequent drawings, however crude they may be.

Anyone wishing to make a serious study of grasses

should prepare an herbarium, that is, a collection of plants pressed and dried in such a way that they may be mounted by gummed straps to sheets of heavy paper and arranged in folders for reference. Grasses so prepared keep indefinitely. A circular giving "Directions for preparing herbarium specimens of Grasses" (Bureau of Plant Industry Document 442, 1909) may be obtained without charge on request to the office of the Systematic Agrostologist, Bureau of Plant Industry, United States Department of Agriculture, Washington, D. C.

In studying grasses the first thing is to understand the structure of the plant in hand, particularly its inflorescence; the second is to learn its relationship to other grasses and what name has been applied to it. The latter is what is meant by "identifying" or "determining" a plant. Practically all the grasses of the United States are described in one or more manuals of botany or state floras. Most of these manuals give "keys" to genera and species. [The word key is used figuratively—an instrument by means of which a way is opened.] A key is an arrangement of contrasting characters by which, choosing one and rejecting the other, the student is led to the name which applies to the plant in hand. For example, take Figs. 23, 27, 45, 48, 65, and 76, and trace them through the following key, reading both of the lines having like indention, these giving the contrasting characters from which to choose.

Spikelets laterally compressed, the florets falling from the persistent glumes.
  Inflorescence a panicle, spikelets pediceled.
    Plants diœcious; spikelets several-flowered..... DISTICHLIS.
    Plants perfect; spikelets 1-flowered............... STIPA.
  Inflorescence a spike, spikelets sessile.
    Spike solitary; spikelets several-flowered, borne on opposite sides of the rachis.......................... LOLIUM.
    Spikes several, digitate; spikelets 1-flowered, borne on one side of the rachis.......................... CAPRIOLA.
Spikelets dorsally compressed, the spikelets falling entire or together with joints of the rachis.
  Spikelets all alike, solitary (borne singly) on a continuous rachis................................ AXONOPUS.
  Spikelets of two kinds borne in pairs, one sessile and perfect, the other pediceled and sterile, the rachis articulated................................ ANDROPOGON.

In actual work, of course, one never has so simple a problem as that. With exceptions (such as are noted pages 44 and 59) and closely related genera and species, it often demands careful weighing of all the facts to use an extended key successfully, but it is excellent training in judgment.

The name reached in the key is verified or rejected by reading the description in the text and noting how the characters of the plant agree with those specified. When the description does not apply to the plant in hand, one must return to the key and try again.

BOOKS

The plants one obtains for himself, and he studies them by means of the few tools mentioned before (p. 6). To identify the plants requires books.

A recently published work, "The Genera of Grasses of the United States," by A. S. Hitchcock, Bulletin 772, United States Department of Agriculture, giving keys to tribes and genera, descriptions and illustrations of all the genera, and notes on the more important species, as well as indications of exceptions, most helpful to the beginner, is the first book which the student should acquire. It may be obtained from the Superintendent of Documents, Government Printing Office, Washington, D. C., at 40 cents a copy. The farmer, the agricultural student, or the botanist who wishes only to be able to identify any conspicuous or useful, weedy or injurious grass of his neighborhood requires nothing more than this and the manual of botany covering his region. The following are the current manuals:

From Maine to Virginia and west to Minnesota and Missouri, inclusive: Gray's New Manual of Botany, 7th edition, 1908 (grasses, by A. S. Hitchcock); Britton's Manual of the Flora of the Northern States and Canada, 3d edition, 1907 (grasses, by G. V. Nash), extending west to the western boundary of Kansas and Nebraska; Britton and Brown's Illustrated Flora of the Northern United States, Canada, and the British Possessions, second edition,

1913, 3 volumes (grasses, by G. V. Nash, in volume 1).

From North Carolina to Florida and west to Oklahoma and Texas: Small's Flora of the Southeastern United States, 1903 (grasses, by G. V. Nash).

The Rocky Mountain region and east to the Black Hills of South Dakota: Coulter and Nelson's New Manual of Botany of the Central Rocky Mountains, 1909 (this does not cover the Mexican flora that extends into southern New Mexico and Arizona); Rydberg's Flora of the Rocky Mountains and Adjacent Plains, 1917.

There is no manual covering the flora of the Southwest, but Wooton and Standley's Flora of New Mexico (Contributions United States National Herbarium, Vol. 19, 1915), includes also most of the species of Arizona. This work gives keys to the genera and species and descriptions of the genera but not of the species.

California: Jepson's Flora of California, 1912. (Grasses, by A. S. Hitchcock).

Washington: Piper's Flora of the State of Washington (Contributions United States National Herbarium, Vol. 11, 1906), giving keys but not descriptions; Piper and Beattie's Flora of the Northwestern Coast, 1915, with keys and descriptions; and Piper and Beattie's Flora of Southeastern Washington and adjacent Idaho, 1914, with keys and descriptions.

Oregon, Utah, and Nevada, and most of Idaho

are not yet covered by manuals, but manuals of adjoining regions include most of the species.

Besides these general manuals there are: Hitchcock's Text-Book of Grasses, 1914, with illustrations, treating of economic grasses and their uses and also of the morphology and the classification of grasses; Grasses of Iowa, Part II, by Pammel, Ball, and Scribner (Iowa Geological Survey, Supplementary Report, 1905), with keys, descriptions, and illustrations; Grasses of Illinois, by Edna Mosher (University of Illinois Agricultural Experiment Station Bulletin 205, 1918), with keys, descriptions, and illustrations; Manual of Farm Grasses, by A. S. Hitchcock, 1921.

A helpful little bulletin is Lyman Carrier's "Identification of Grasses by Their Vegetative Characters" (Bulletin 461, United States Department of Agriculture, to be obtained from the Superintendent of Documents, Government Printing Office, Washington, D. C., for 5 cents). One should always have the inflorescence for accurate identification, but there are occasions when one would be glad to identify a seedling if possible.

One who finds interest and delight in the study of grasses will want to accumulate a working library. A bibliography of even the most important works would be too long to be included here and would be out of place in a first book of grasses. However, it may be well to mention a number of papers on grasses that have been issued in the past few years by the United States Department of Agriculture and the United States National Herbarium which can be purchased for a small amount from the Superintendent of Documents or, the few out of print, from dealers in second-hand books.

Hitchcock, A. S. North American Species of Leptochloa. U. S. Dept. Agr., Bur. Pl. Ind. Bull. 33, 24 pp., with plates. 1903.

North American Species of Agrostis. U. S. Dept. Agr., Bur. Pl. Ind. Bull. 68, 68 pp., with plates. 1905.

Mexican Grasses in the United States National Herbarium. Contr. U. S. Nat. Herb. 17, pp. 181–389. 1913.

The North American Species of Ichnanthus; The North American Species of Lasiacis. Contr. U. S. Nat. Herb. 22, 31 pp., with plates. 1920.

Revisions of North American Grasses: Isachne, Oplismenus, Echinochloa, and Chaetochloa. Contr. U. S. Nat. Herb. 22, pp. 115–208, with text figures. 1920.

and Chase, Agnes. The North American Species of Panicum. Contr. U. S. Nat. Herb. 15, 396 pp., with text figures. 1910.

Tropical North American Species of Panicum. Contr. U. S. Nat. Herb. 17, pp. 459–539, with text figures. 1915.

Grasses of the West Indies. Contr. U. S. Nat. Herb. 18, pp. 261–471. 1917.

Griffiths, David. The Grama Grasses: Bouteloua and Related Genera. Contr. U. S. Nat. Herb. 14, pp. 343–428, with plates. 1912.

Merrill, Elmer D. North American Species of Spartina. U. S. Dept. Agr., Bur. Pl. Ind. Bull. 9, 16 pp. 1902.

Piper, C. V. North American Species of Festuca. Contr. U. S. Nat. Herb. 10, 48 pp., with plates. 1906.

Scribner, F. L., and Merrill, E. D. The Grasses of Alaska. Contr. U. S. Nat. Herb. 13, pp. 47–92. 1910.

Shear, C. L. A Revision of the North American Species of Bromus Occurring North of Mexico. U. S. Dept. Agr. Div. Agrost. Bull. 23, 66 pp., with text figures. 1900.

Chase, Agnes. The North American Species of Brachiaria; The North American Species of Cenchrus. Contr. U. S. Nat. Herb. 22, pp. 33–77, with text figures. 1920.

The North American Species of Pennisetum. Contr. U. S., Nat. Herb. 22, pp. 209–234, with text figures. 1921.

BOTANICAL NAMES

In the introduction, the reasons were given for using Latin names of plants. It will have been noticed that these names are made up of two words, the generic name (a noun) and the specific (an adjective or a noun in the possessive case or in apposition), and that the generic name is placed first, like the surnames of persons in a directory.

Both words of the name are generally supposed to refer to some characteristic or property of the plant to which it is applied, as Lepturus (slender tail) cylindricus (cylindric) and Erianthus (woolly flower) saccharoides (like Saccharum, that is, sugar-cane), but often botanical names do not fit any better than do names of persons—Paul (meaning small) Baker may be a tall blacksmith, or Martha (meaning bitter) Stern may be sweet and gentle. Many of the Linnæan genera bear the ancient classic Greek or Latin names, such as Quercus for the oak and Ulmus for the elm. In many other cases Linnæus used classic names but applied them, not as anciently used, but to a different group. Bromus to the Greeks was the oat, but Linnæus used it for the brome-grasses; Zizanion was the tares (supposed to be *Lolium temulentum*) sown by the enemy among the wheat, in the parable of Scripture, but Linnæus used the feminine form of the word for our wild rice. On the whole, however, botanical names are more or less descriptive, and it is helpful as well as interesting to be mindful of their meaning, especially of the names of species. Any plant with the name "asper" or "scaber" will be rough in some part; "pubescens" will be hairy; "alba" will have white flowers or bark probably, and "rubra" red. The name *Bromus secalinus* implies that the species was a weed in the rye (Secale) fields of Europe, as it is in our wheat fields. *Holcus halepensis* was known in the early ages from Aleppo (Haleb) in Syria, and *Phalaris canariensis* from the Canary Islands.

The present system of botanical nomenclature dates from 1753, when Linnæus's Species Plantarum was published, using binomials (names of two words) for all the species. Before this, plants were given phrase names, more or less descriptive, such as "Panicum with lax drooping panicle, the sheaths of the leaves pubescent," for proso millet (*Panicum miliaceum*) or "Grass with a very long spike, like cat-tail," for timothy. These phrase names were in Latin, of course. Linnæus's binomial plan so simplified the hitherto cumbersome system that it was everywhere adopted in less than a generation.

In botanical works it will be noted that plant names are followed by the initial, abbreviation, or the full name of a person, as *Poa pratensis* L., *Phragmites communis* Trin. This stands for the name of the person who gave the plant the name, L. for Linnæus, Trin. for Trinius. It has often happened that the same species has been given different names by men working in various places and not in touch with each other. In such cases the name first given is the one now generally used. It has also happened that two species in a genus have been given the same name. In this case the name stands for the earlier one and the second is renamed. These superabundant names constitute what is termed synonymy. (Synonyms are two or more names for the same thing.) Superabundant names are also due to the fact that many species when first described were placed in genera to which more intensive study shows they do not belong. *Triodia flava*, for example, was first named *Poa flava* by Linnæus, and *Danthonia spicata* was named *Avena spicata* by him. When these species are placed in Triodia and Danthonia, respectively, the name of the original author is given in parenthesis with the name or abbreviation of the person who made the change following it; thus, *Triodia flava* (L.) Hitchc., *Danthonia spicata* (L.) DC.

CLASSIFICATION OF PLANTS

As stated in the introduction (page 2), the classification of grasses is based on the characters of the spikelet. The classification of plants is itself but a human attempt to show natural relationship, and the attempt is based on knowledge of but an infinitesimal part of the plant kingdom. The plants occupying the earth today are the survivors of millions of generations. Countless forms have become extinct. Some of these are known from fossils, but far more have vanished, leaving no record. Linnæus said "Nature never makes jumps." Connecting links exist or have existed between the greatest extremes. When no such link is known, we conjecture that the missing intermediates are among the countless extinct forms. Human minds approaching a given problem from various angles form different conjectures; hence it is, that botanists of different periods or even of the same period, have diverse ideas of relationships. The species that Linnæus described under Poa, for example, are today recognized as belonging in three genera and his species of Panicum in nine genera. As a vastly greater number of plants are known today, botanists have wider knowledge on which to base conclusions, but the main difference between the Linnæan and the present-day idea of genera is due to the modern concept of a genus as a network of related species as contrasted with the earlier concept of a genus as a sort of receptacle built of certain characters and open to any species having those characters. Linnæus's idea of Cenchrus, for example, was primarily a genus of bur-grasses, and, besides what is now recognized as Cenchrus (represented by Figs. 70 and 71), he included in it a species of Nazia (Fig. 54) and a Mediterranean grass in which the "bur" is composed of the rigid lobes of the lemmas of the dense head of spikelets, as well as a plant that is not a grass.

This brief explanation is offered to save the beginner undue bewilderment when he finds in using different books that the standard excuse offered by botanists of all times and places, that the Latin name of a plant is the same throughout the world, is not as true as could be wished.

It will be noted in using botanical works that certain characters are accepted as generic, that is, as indicating that species having these characters in common belong to a single genus. Such are the 5-nerved keeled lemmas of Poa. Other characters, sometimes quite as conspicuous, such as the pubescence or want of it in Poa, and the presence or absence of an awn in Bromus and Festuca, are regarded as specific, that is, as differentiating species. It might seem as though by some revelation certain characters are known to be generic and others to be specific. Such is not the case. A species consists of a group of individuals presumably capable of freely inter-breeding. A genus is a group of species which in the sum total of their characters are so much alike as to warrant the assumption that they have had a common ancestor. Characters taken as generic and specific are analogous to theories or working hypotheses. We use them as far as they work; if they do not work, we discard them for other characters. Botany is a science of living things, and its problems can never be settled once for all. It is this enduring interest that makes it so fascinating.

POSITION OF GRASSES IN THE PLANT KINGDOM

Flowering plants (excluding the pines and their allies) fall into two rather distinct groups, (1) monocotyledons, characterized by an embryo having a single cotyledon and by stems having woody fibers not in layers but distributed through them (as seen in the cornstalk) and not increasing in thickness by age, and (2) dicotyledons, with an embryo having two cotyledons and stems with their woody fibers forming a zone between pith and bark and increasing in thickness by annual layers. Cotyledons are the seed leaves. Anyone will have observed that sprouting corn, rye, and other grasses send up a single leaf first, while squash, radishes, lettuce, and morning-glories, for example, have a pair of opposite seed leaves. Grasses belong in the first class, with sedges, rushes, lilies, and the like. They form a highly specialized family with a greater number of species than any other except the orchids and the composites (asters, dandelions, thistles, and their kinds).

Grasses have been so successful in the struggle for existence that they have a wider range than any other family, occupying all parts of the earth and exceeding any other in the number of individuals. They reach the limits of vegetation (except for lichens and algæ) in the polar regions and on mountain tops, endure both cold and torrid desert conditions, form the main part of the vegetation of vast prairies, plains, savannas, and steppes of both hemispheres, and occupy great stretches of marsh and tide flats, where they are building up dry land. Bamboos, the largest of grasses, form extensive forests and dense jungles. Grasses range in height from less than an inch, full grown, to over a hundred feet, and they have developed all manner of contrivances for the dissemination of their seeds.

GRASSES IN RELATION TO MAN

Of all plants, grasses are by far the most important to man. The grains of wheat, barley, rye, oats, rice, corn, sorghum, and millet form the staple food of the greater part of mankind, while the animals that furnish food and labor, wool, mohair, and leather live principally on grasses. The grains are also sources of starch, alcohol, and glucose. Sugar and sirup are obtained from sugar-cane and varieties of sorghum, and of late years enormous quantities of cooking oil are secured from the germ of the corn. Grasses furnish the material for brooms and brushes and are an important source of fiber for paper-making and cordage. Tons of essential oils used in perfumeries are annually extracted from grasses. In a great part of Asia and Oceanica bamboo forms the principal or only timber for buildings and bridges and furnishes the material for all manner of tools, utensils, and furniture.

INDEX